AF644292

SUCCESS STARTS IN **YOUR HEART**

Spirit Flows Power Glows

notionpress
.com

SUCCESS STARTS IN **YOUR HEART**

Spirit Flows Power Glows

Keerthi Singhe

notionpress.com

Notion Press

Old No. 38, New No. 6

McNichols Road, Chetpet

Chennai - 600 031

First Published by Notion Press 2015

Copyright © Keerthi singhe 2015

All Rights Reserved.

ISBN 978-93-5206-457-1

This book has been published in good faith that the work of the author is original. All efforts have been taken to make the material error-free. However, the author and the publisher disclaim the responsibility.

No part of this book may be reproduced or transmitted in any form or by any means, graphic, electronic, or mechanical, including photocopying, recording, taping, or by any information storage retrieval system, without the permission, in writing, from the publisher.

Dedication

I have two shareholders in my life's enterprise who have invested their genes in me - my father, who is in heaven, and my mother, who waits to see me bounce back. Who else can I present this book to, but them?

Contents

Preface

The Great Witnesses of God! My belief

You will be strengthened and powered, according to your belief, on whoever it may be. It may be God, religion, the power of the Universe, or whatever you believe in as eternal virtues.

My finger tips began to move to write the content of my manuscript with God given spirit and enthusiasm. The 'Creativity' rights of this book go to God, while its copyrights go to me. Without His Godly direction, this book wouldn't have been crafted and completed so beautifully, so all credits go to Him, and the rest I put in His hands before your hands.

Have you ever experienced the living God? He came to me and saved my soul in His time. I had been waiting for Him over a long period; sometimes He came and sometimes He went by. He didn't stay with me all the time.

I started various vivid things in my life, which prevailed for months or a few years and then disappeared from my possession, released from my grip.

I had all the luxuries that I wished for. My heart believes that all these things were supplied by God.

But when I was unable to stay away from ungodly practices, God distanced Himself from me. Again hard times began to haunt me.

I cried out to God, and He answered my prayers and saved me. But He didn't give me more than I needed.

I tried a number of things for living, and for a period of time, they gave me fruits.

When I meandered into ungodly ways, I suffered low results or no results at all.

Recently I decided to go to the house of the Lord and celebrate Him. A few days back, before I began to write this book, I fell badly sick and was hospitalized.

The Doctors told me that I had swine flu and pneumonia. I had been suffering from high fever, my mouth was filled with ulcers and I was not able to eat anything. I thought that I was going to die.

I made a vow of sacrifice and expressed my joy to God.

My vow became a 'wow'!

The Specialists and Doctors were amazed as the reports became normal. I received marvelous energy, as God healed me miraculously.

I started going towards my dreams, He sharpened my talents and gave me wisdom in His time.

I have been experiencing miracles in my life, all the time. God is holding me tight in His embrace.

I am celebrating His glory as He makes me shine.

The Art of Bouncing Back

In writing this book, I have captured unforgettable, painful, yet interesting memories and incidents that are stored in my life, blending them with the principles of success that I have learned through successful characters. I have applied and have experienced them. The results are tremendously guaranteed if you apply those result oriented practices, and develop yourself internally and externally. Internal development is reconditioning your mindset through mind exercises, such as prayers, affirmations, meditation and the reading of goals. Externally, you can find your talents and develop your skill towards competency, and build relationships. When you use those principles of success, enjoy them as an art, not as arduous rules.

I experienced many failures, one after the other. It was very tough to bear the harsh consequences that failures offered me in the past. To initiate something fresh is easy, but it is hard to raise our heads again when we are cowed down by the circumstances and situations even once. When we fail sometimes, we lose all the material resources we have, along with our self confidence, in most cases. Our ability to think clearly vanishes. The hardest part is reconditioning our mind set. First we have to rearrange our mind; otherwise, pouring water into a leaky bucket is futile.

People who have enjoyed super success in their lives, have failed several times and regained in thousand folds what they lost. They have played with failure, which has acted as a great impetus in their lives. Many give up when the shadows of failure peep in, without confronting them physically.

It took me seven years to clarify my life's purpose, and analyze my potentialities to fight back in my life, after a great failure I encountered in 2008. For the last six months, I have been associating with successful personalities with their written and audio literatures. They have pumped into me the oxygen to breathe again. Today I use the laws and principles of success they used.

In order to conserve your valuable biological age and use it productively, I recommend that one should get in touch with successful characters as soon as possible. It is not easy to physically meet them, as some are no more.

The easy and most economical way is through books, seminars and conferences, audio and video programs that are easily available within your reach.

'Spirit flows, Power glows' is written in simple language and enhanced with all my true life experiences.

In every chapter, you will find something interesting and something easy to keep in your memory. It's up to you, as you can start reading from any chapter and grasp the essence.

Why did I take seven years to bounce back? The reason is the lack of knowledge of the Arts outlined in this book. You will not find those ingredients as rules separately, yet they are mixed bountifully in my recipe in each and every chapter. Would you be happy if I tell you that you can take only seven days to read this book, assimilate its ingredients and stand with amazing courage to pursue your dreams? Remember to discipline yourself to go through this book several times because discipline is one of the vital keys to unlock all other rooms of success.

I believe that I could address the consciousness of common people in this literature. After all, it is your obligation to become what you want to be in future.

Thank you very much for buying this book and I hope you would extend your hand to someone else to make one's life colorful.

Keerthisinghe

Acknowledgements

Special thanks to Leiya P Kharei for the extended immense motivation, inspiration and support.

Dinethra Uthsala Wijerathne, my son who is the driving force behind me, and I owe this all to him...

Eroshmi Davina Fernando who helped me in different ways when I was in downturn...

Karu Jayasooriya (Hon' speaker of the Parliament of Sri Lanka), an amazing leader I respect the most for his Leadership Qualities and is down to earth personality.

All authors

Dalai Lama, Dr. Norman Vincent Peale, John C. Maxwell, Les Brown, Brian Tracy, Dr. Joseph Murphy, Napoleon Hill, Jack Canfield, Louis Hay- They are my inspirational mentors, though I haven't met them in person.

Freddy, for the help in editing this.

Babita Singh

Pastor John & Karuna Prakasam

P. Vijitha Thero, Nalin Wijeratna, Sanjeewa Senivirathna, Siddeek, Thushara Jayawardane, Jc Alawathuwala, Sujith Pererra, Sujeewa Senasinghe, Buddy (Rohana), Atula, Hari, Mary Karlson, Kimiyo Kondo, Sachiko, Nana, Teresa, John, Jojo.

Viki, Mark Lei, Sumit & Tanya, TJ, Karan, Chi, Manoj Bhatt, Manoj Yadav Gurnam, H.P. Singh, Anil Virmani, Sanjeev Virmani, Bhai.

Notion press.

All my supporters and well-wishers around the world.

1

Vision Code

The greater the vision you have in mind, the grander the things you experience in life as a reality.

Keerthisinghe

How do you visualize? In order to give you an idea, I will write my vision code in this chapter. I see my future in all areas of life, finance, career, health and fitness, freedom, relations, personal goals and social contributions in perfect detail. I add emotions and feelings as ingredients to evoke and provoke my memory. Get a guide line and envision your future, so that it can stand before you as a reality.

I have my protein powder shake and all the food supplements provided by my loving wife. I pick some fruits and nuts from the colorful fruit platter on the tray. I can hear the laughter of my grandchildren. They are awake already and playing with my son, who is reading his newspapers in the lobby. In fact, we get up every day, hearing their laughter which resonates everywhere in our home. My grandchildren peep into our room and greet us for the day.

"Good morning, grandpa, grandma." Not just once, but again and again. They jump on our bed and hug us, and again jump down from the bed, until their mother comes and takes them to the bathroom.

Now I am in my bathroom, which is one of my favorite places to be, at least around one hour a day. It's very spacious, and was designed by a famous architect and made with luxurious amenities. Gold plated frames, hangings and some precious stones are studded in the Jacuzzi tub and the mirror. I like the new fragrance; I can't make it out exactly what aroma it is because it's changed several times a day by my housekeeping staff. It invigorates me, as light and relaxing music plays. I am thinking of writing my new book, sitting on the couch near the Jacuzzi. New ideas always come to my mind when I spend time in my rest room. Sometimes I practice my speeches inside the rest room.

Through a big window I can see nature's beauty in my garden, with birds on the well grown mango trees. On some days, peacocks and deer can be seen in my garden. The paintings which hang on the walls were recently bought at an auction in France. We flew to France last month specially to participate in the grand antique auction.

I stand in front of the mirror. My hair is completely gray. "You still have enough hair to comb," I tell myself. I think my forehead has widened. I stretch my arms, look at my chest area and tummy still looking strong and healthy in shape. For a long time my waist size has been thirty four.

I affirm my affirmations. "Keerthi, I love you; you are a wonderful gift of God. You are always creative and a happy being. Today is one of the best days in your life. Everything is going to happen in your best favor." I feel energetic; all areas of my life bring me joy. I am whole and complete, as I have contributed many things to my country and the world. I am still trying to motivate my fellow citizens in the globe through my books and motivational speeches. I notice my assistants are observing my movements inside the bathroom without disturbing me. Even though I can do things by myself, my son has deployed them for my safety. The bathroom floor and amenities have been covered with specially made rubber, to ensure that, even if I fall down, no harm will occur. I'm in my eighties. I enjoy shaving by myself. I also enjoy the Jacuzzi for around twenty minutes.

After a bath, I go to my wardrobe where my entire collection of clothes is stored. My favorite clothes are lying in the dry cleaned section and all the others are brand new. It's larger than a departmental store. Jackets, shirts, trousers, shoes, belts, watches in all the top brands in the world, are in my home. My costume designer and assistants help me to dress according to the occasion. They bring ties to match my suit.

Around 8AM, I go to have my breakfast, and all are waiting until I arrive - my wife, sons, daughters and grandchildren. The buffet includes Continental and my favorite, typical Sri Lankan food. While having breakfast, my son talks about some political affairs with me. After an hour long breakfast, my son rushes to his political office by his own helicopter and it takes only 20 minutes. I go to my business office where I can monitor all its activities online.

In my office I have three sections; one is my online market place, *www.hitbazzar.com* which is a multibillion dollar business where I have offices and operations in many countries. The head office is located in India, and once a month I visit it. The second is my motivational speech department.

I check the invitations for my speeches, and I meet my co workers and assistant trainers. The last one is my book store. In my dashboard, I can see all the data of my books, audio and video tapes that are for sale. I spend two hours there.

Around 10.30 am I go to my home spa. I spend around two hours, and experience my favorite herbal compressor massage with aroma body therapy. If needed, I get a haircut and facial, along with a pedicure and manicure. My spa has the best female therapists in the world; some are full timers and others come visiting, according to our family requirements.

I spend most of the time, if I am in the country, in one of my favorite houses located in the ancient kingdom, Anuradhapura, Sri Lanka. From my house, I can see all the big stupas in the pooja city. My home faces the Nuwarawewa lake and is situated in the hundred acre land, where all the facilities are available in the house. Tennis courts, both indoor and outdoor, mini theater, gym, guest houses, restaurants, cafes and a boutique hotel! The boutique hotel is not open to everyone. Guests can come by invitations only.

Every day I go to the floor where my collection of cars is parked and I enjoy a short ride in one of my favorite cars. All the best brands of the world are available in my fleet. My grandchildren love to give me company. Also we are expecting the new arrivals and my grandchildren are anxiously waiting to see the cars that I had bought in new auctions from different countries of the world recently.

On Sundays, our main task is to host the church service, and facilitate a five star lunch for all the guests. I enjoy this activity more than all the other routines in the day. All our family members usually attend. Praising the Lord for His grants is the most enjoyable thing in life. Apart from the lunch we host, every day in the evening, free breads are served for needy families at the stall located near the main entrance of the house.

These days my wife is busy choosing places for our next vacation. Most of the time, we all go together as a family. This time I prefer to go to Bali Islands where we own our own grand villa.

Once a month we host a dinner with my friends, politicians, diplomats and business people among the crowd. They enjoy our bar and multi cuisine restaurants. Most of the time, we watch movies together in our theater. They enjoy the best wines we serve while watching movies.

This year again I was ranked as one of the top five speakers in the world and the ceremony is to be held in Vegas. I will be interviewed by CNN and a guest lecture is scheduled in the coming December in Harvard.

Highlights

I am happy being the number one .... in Sri Lanka by 2030. My son is standing next to me. We signed agreements for major...............

I celebrate being... .... in Sri Lanka by 2034. My mother is in the first row among the guests.

My son becomes .... by 2046, and I revel in this moment as a proud father.

My world is limitless and powerful. I see no stop signs; my life is flowing like water and takes shape according to my containers. Nobody can stop me, as I'm Unstoppable. I have a well balanced and very successful life.

In order to carry a positive action we must develop here a positive vision.

Dalai Lama

Vision is the art of seeing what is invisible to others.

Jonathan Swift

The one thing that you have that nobody else has is you. Your voice, your mind, your story, your vision. So write and draw and build and play and dance and live as only you can.

Neil Gaiman

The only thing worse than being blind is having sight but no vision.

Helen Keller

Where there is no vision, there is no hope.

George Washington Carve

2

Will to do it

Do you have any specific will in your life?

The dictionary gives us the meaning of our will.

The capability of conscious choice and decision and intention!

It is combined with three important and very forceful success norms; choice, decision and intention.

It simply says that if you have the will to do and achieve something, you are willful and impulsive. You have got driven forces within. Let me come up with my own life stories to give you a better understanding.

In 2004, I contested the assembly elections in North Central Province, Sri Lanka. When I made an application to the party to get a nomination for candidature to the Assembly, I was summoned before the nomination board, which consisted of all party bigwigs. I hadn't seen most of them before and I felt a bit nervous, but I was able to manage it through my desire. It was not an ordinary desire to contest in this election. I dreamt big and imagined my success at the top of the ladder. I was astute enough to wear a dress for the interview which was almost the same style as that the party leader used to wear. A tunic with long white sleeves, shirt tucked in properly into cream trousers, brown shoes and belt. Sometimes we have to impress people, scrutinizing their preferences and tastes to offer emotional bribes. It doesn't harm anyone, but only pushes them to feel that you are like minded. People like to work or cooperate with similar type of characters; outwardly, first impressions work. You will never get a second chance to impress someone. First impressions are long lasting.

I said, "Good morning, Sirs!"

The party leader glanced at me and observed me properly. It was like a quick scanning, and he said,

"I am very happy to see young leaders like you and your interest in our party affairs. We appreciate it, but sorry, there is no space in the nomination list for you. It's full. You applied for your nominations at the last moment.

You can come next time. You have enough time, and during that time, you can do some work for the party and get some experience."

I didn't have any idea about national politics and I had not contested local government elections either. I said, "Sir, I prefer to be nominated this time."

"Why are you in a hurry? Any reason?"

I said I possessed the will to do it! He looked at me from top to bottom, and then, I saw a glow on his face. "What kind of will do you have? Can you explain a bit?" I clearly observed him as he turned to the deputy leader's side. He sat next to him and gave him a smile. I said, "Sir, in 1962, when John F Kennedy proclaimed that he would send man to the moon, he had the will to do it. There were no people to send, no resources, no budget. But they did it.

He said, "Fine, but the list is full and one candidate who was recommended by our district leader, is on his way. If he doesn't come, you might get a chance. Wait outside for a few hours."

Hours passed, and my supporters were disappointed; they came up with different ideas and strategies to get the consent from the district leaders. I told my supporters to wait until the party leader called me again. The party's district bigwigs were all against me. The reason was that I was new, young and quite rich. There were rumors around the district that I was very rich and had seven ships. It was not true but financially, I was in good shape. I had bought a new jeep to use specially for election purposes. These rumors caused some sort of fear among the bigwigs of the party in the district.

I waited until two o'clock the next day. I was called again before the nomination board and the party leader said, "Young man, again I should remind you that all the party bigwigs in the district are not willing to give you a chance. You will be at risk of defeat as it will be a hard contest. Besides, you will have to put in much effort and spend money."

I replied, "Sir, I like it. Why is it going to be hard and risky? I had a practical plan for the campaign. They endorsed my nomination as a stand by guy. It meant if that candidate who was supposed to come had come next day again, I would have had to keep quiet and my name would have been erased from the list."

Anyway, he didn't come. My burning desire, blended with my practical plan of action, boosted by my creative intelligence, attracted all the resource people and contacts to my doorstep.

If you have the will to do it, you will be willful and impulsive, and find ways creatively to make it a success. Will involves active force because it's involved with decision and intention. When you decide to choose something, you have a choice and you will never lose. The choice will be good and you will get the fruits, if you allow it to flow after finding your life's purpose. I believe my purpose in life is to serve people.

After one month, the election was held and the stand by guy became number one in the province. It was big news in the party because I was the stand by guy. The three senior guys lost badly. Our party became the opposition in the provincial council, and out of twenty one local government bodies, nineteen requested my party leader to appoint me as an opposition leader of the province. But due to the opposition by district leaders, he couldn't do it. I was given many responsibilities by the party which normally parliamentarians get, due to my brilliant start which reflected my will.

I believe and have experienced that super achievements do not merely come with the knowledge that you possess, the experience that you gained or from strategies that you implemented. They come from within, from a burning desire and by imagining vivid pictures that arouse your creative intelligence.

3

Create your design

Memory holds you back, imagination pushes you forward.

Keerthisinghe

Paint your picture, paint your life. How do you picture yourself? You can paint your picture vividly, and manifest it according to whom you want to show up as, in this world. Think about the Great Artists who gifted valuable arts to this planet; their creativity came to the surface as they thought they were great. Great leaders, Inventors, Architects, Writers, Speakers, Financial Emperors, and Spiritual Leaders who have created their own identities, have used their creative intelligence which possessed infinite creativity. All human beings have creativity in their creative faculty which is hidden in the subconscious mind. The conscious mind is not creative, but objective. You think from your conscious mind, you sit for your exam, follow a training course, read a book, find a partner, buy a home, find a job; you can consciously think and do all these.

Many people become complete machines, using only the conscious part of their mind. It is very limited and they feel exhausted, stressed, tired and bored. Then they temporarily find some solutions to relax their mind and body. Many people who have limited resources, limited money, limited time and freedom do not use their creative faculty. They don't create anything for themselves or for this world. We have to do something for our living; you can see some people who rise in their respective fields by using creativity as a strategy. Regardless of the type of organization, they create ideas, design some action plans, create some structures and move forward. They are creating positions for themselves. They are not going after positions; positions are coming after them. In fact, not only positions, but fame will pursue them. Once you find your own creativity, it doesn't let you sleep eight to ten hours a day, or play all the time with your electronic gadgets or social media sites to kill your valuable time. Creativity has life. It's breathing; it makes a sound always and gets attention, multiplies your fruits, enhances your capacity and transcends you. Use this amazing faculty in life.

In order to create something that you really want in life, you have to have passion. If you are passionate about something, you will clearly feel something in your heart, with tremendous energy, happiness, joy, which you will entertain when you possess it in the real world. When it becomes very strong emotion, you consciously decide to act towards your desired task constantly. Your mind will see the colorful pictures of your end results. When that picture transfers and deposits in your subconscious mind, its creative faculty will be energized and activated. Sometimes you may feel that you have a bunch of ideas. Don't even let one of them to go into your trash. Write them down in a paper and put them somewhere safely. When you need them, you can go through them carefully, pump oxygen into them and give them life. It will help you to create something extraordinary and set foot in the next level of your life.

I notice, on many occasions in my life, that I have a great force in me that other ordinary people don't possess. How it can be? I am also just a simple human being. Not only me, you also will get these kind of feelings and thoughts if you earnestly analyze them. It's not just the motivation. I believe when we have those kinds of feeling, our souls connect with the creator of all. According to me, He is my God. Because of His power, I possess an amazing power within. Some people think it's a universal power. When I have that great force in me, it is very creative. If I write something or act on it, it gives me incredibly big results and amazes me. Sometimes when I read what I wrote, I wonder where I got the content and facts, and how I wrote them.

"The doctor dresses the wound, and God heals it."

An old saying

You have to do the preliminary things with great enthusiasm by yourself, and the end result will follow through superior help from above.

Creativity gets life through imagination. When you imagine something, impressions will be stay in your brain cells, and your subjective mind will find the path to create what you really want. If you don't imagine anything, you will never create anything. The future, wealth, happiness; you have to create them; barring this, you will lead an average life and leave the planet with unused talents. Many people have a tendency to create limitations for themselves. They limit and make their boundaries, mentally and physically. They flounder with invalid reasons created by themselves. But they don't have an idea about that. The majority of people face this situation and become neutral. You can see very low energy people who merely exist because they were born. They don't think that they are born to win; they think that they are born to lose. They don't like their lives, faces, physical appearances and what they do for their living. Just like walking skeletons! Why are many people not creative? Don't they have creativity within? It is just that they don't have the will to create something extraordinary. They are content with the things which others created and they just become wanderers or followers. They don't consciously think about innovative ideas. The subconscious mind is subjective; it has creative intelligence, but doesn't have reasoning power and it can't work against your will. Will is your capability of conscious choice, decision and intention. When you lack the choice, decision and intention to create something, your creative intelligence remains in a coma.

One slogan that I coined brought me a huge victory in my political campaign. In my language ***"Dasa raja dam, Yali osawam"*** means, "I will bring back the **Dasa-Raja-Dhamma: The 'Ten Royal Virtues** that a king should possess when he rules his kingdom," a dictum preached by Lord Buddha.

How to be creative: Start small; there are occasions when we have to create something for living, or need to come out when we encounter particular situations or circumstances. I once rented out a hotel in New Delhi, specifically to provide accommodation for Sri Lankan Buddhist pilgrims who wanted to worship Buddhist places in India. They were transiting Delhi and I facilitated quality accommodation as compared to the other places they had stayed in earlier. I created that because I had the will to do so.

I had to send money for my son's education. It was necessary. Unless I offered something different, I would have had to face the competition badly. I also opened a Sari (Traditional Dress) shop inside the hotel premises and created a marketing strategy to maximize the sales, preventing pilgrims from going to other places in the bazaar.

I noticed that they wanted to buy at least one good thing, of high quality, as a souvenir of their tour. I created that opportunity. I went to the fabric manufacturer and got quality materials which were not available in the bazaar, made saris and put up a sign board, "If you buy one, you will get five free." When they bought that expensive sari, I gave them five ordinary saris which were available in the market. Five free, all were happy! I earned sufficient money to send to my family.

When you create small things in the beginning, it becomes a habitual action. Then you will be able to create something big according to your conscious requirements, because you have impressed a message as a strong signal in your subconscious mind, the message being, **"I am creative."**

You must have noticed, all of a sudden, that you get a creative idea which you have never ever thought of. How did it evolve? As a result of your will, your subjective mind created it, processing and analyzing your thoughts which had passed down to your subconscious mind previously.

Memory count

1. Be creative and design yourself. God has created your structure; you have to furnish it, by choice, with a good interior and exterior. You have to add value in you.
2. Your experience, observations, training and knowledge are finite and limited. Don't get exhausted using your synthetic faculty. Always find your infinite creative intelligence which will amaze you by giving you exemplary solutions. Most successful people found the creative intelligence within, knowing that they possessed it. Some got great hunches through their creative intelligence unexpectedly.
3. Write down your ideas on a paper and try to develop them. When you have a creative idea, make out a plan based on it, and gather all available sources. Everybody gets creative ideas if they let their minds open up. It's not a unique kind of feature that only successful people taste. To be successful, be creative.
4. Everybody can imagine, some are perceptive and see things in detail, imagining everything which is sensitive to the five senses. You can imagine the smell, sound, feeling, taste and sight. If you are not able see mental pictures, use a vision board which consists of what you want; your dream home, car, vacation, the expected amount of money, everything that you want in your room where you spend most of your time. Make a screen saver in your laptop or smart phone.
5. Never say you are not a creative person; affirm that you are creative. You will become creative.
6. Choose the things that you want, opting for the most magnificent things that ordinary people cannot afford. Have the mental capacity to accept when luxurious things show up in your presence. Don't reject them saying that you are not worthy enough to entertain extravagant things

in your life. Many successful people are self made. They accumulated their riches within their lifetime and not from the previous generations.

7. Create small things in the beginning, and greater things will follow. If you have intense eagerness and enjoyment, greater things can be created in your life.
8. In the process of creating something, you may make some mistakes; however, if you don't stop the process, better things will be created. Create music, create wealth, and create power. It is applicable to all areas. Everything will take a considerable time frame, at least five to seven years or more. Rome was not built in a day.
9. Be passionate; you will have the will power to create things.
10. You will not be able to correct your past, but you can recreate your future. Many make mistakes by trying to correct their past; that is not possible.
11. Create a sketch design of your future in your mind, add expensive and happier things, and organize all your short term and long term activities within the sketch you have designed.
12. If you merely react to the things that are in existence, you will not focus on something new or even expand and develop the existing things. Moving towards creation means, expanding your comfort zone, your attitude, personality and character.

Creativity is allowing yourself to make mistakes. Art is knowing which ones to keep.

Scott Adams

Creativity is putting your imagination to work, and it's produced the most extraordinary results in human culture.

Ken Robinson

Creativity is just connecting things. When you ask creative people how they did something, they feel a little guilty because they didn't really do it, they just saw something. It seemed obvious to them after a while. That's because they were able to connect experiences they've had and synthesize new things.

Steve Jobs

It's impossible to explain creativity. It's like asking a bird, 'How do you fly?' You just do.

Eric Jerome Dickey

I don't see myself as a hero because what I'm doing is self-interested: I don't want to live in a world where there's no privacy and therefore no room for intellectual exploration and creativity.

Edward Snowden

4

Dreamers are True Magnets

Great dreams of great dreamers are always transcended.

A. P. J. Abdul Kalam

Some people have the capacity to live life like uncommon breeds. They represent unique traits that super successful people possess. I prefer to distinguish between successful and super successful people. You can be rich and successful through many ways; even through immoral ways which people follow. If you follow the secrets of success, you can be successful in any area of life you wish to be. Your creative intelligence, which creates abundance, doesn't argue with you as to why you are doing something bad or immoral, because it is under your conscious influence.

Everything is mind; what you think, you become.

Buddha

For him so he thinks in his heart so is he.

Proverbs 23:7

According to the general perception, you can be judged on how you achieve your finance, whether by standards that are ethical, legitimate or not. But super successful people are the people who achieve success in a significant and moral way. They sacrifice many things in life before they go up, always ready to extend their support in different ways. They are others centered. They cast their bread upon the waters. They have big hearts, and have developed moral ethical values even if they don't have college degrees. They draw out, develop within and know how to control their resources, including their master mind groups. They represent integrity, honesty, accountability and loving kindness.

Let me mention a worthy example from the U.S. In1900, Andrew Carnegie became one of the wealthiest persons from scratch, and more than 25 employees became millionaires in his company when he achieved that level. He reproduced richness, proving that his heart was big enough to share and create opportunities for his employees to become rich as well.

Super successful people think in different ways. Their thoughts are ready to reproduce, and their ideas are creative and novel. They are never short of plans. In short, they clothe themselves well, internally and externally. They build their character with laudable qualities of punctuality, unselfishness, trustworthiness, teachability and hopefulness. Their pleasing personality exhibits their desires. When they see you, their eyes speak, and open the doors to enter their endless world. They have infinite intelligence which draws forth all that they need. They never doubt their potentiality. Fear of failure and rejections are not in their diaries. Confidence and abundance are major attributes of their routines. When big dreamers talk, their hearts flow with passion and compassion, which cause you to be inspired yourself. Many of them are truly charismatic and attract others. They are gifted and they have discovered their giftedness. They are ready to give back the investments with profits to this world. They believe that this universe and supernatural powers have helped them to bring up their empires, and they always desire that they should pay back with gratitude for their good fortune.

Check their facial expressions; they never hide success secrets. Notice the confident tone of their voice. Their body language expresses integrity, honesty and firmness. They possess the art of living, often living with style and good humor. Many of them laugh out loud. They open their hearts and live with spirit.

When they walk, they hold their heads up, not downwards, and they take wide steps and bypass you. They never walk slowly and they are not willing to put their hands in their pockets. When they sit or shake hands, they do not bend their heads.

Do you possess any of the traits that I have mentioned above? If not, don't be worried. You can gain and train because most of the successful people don't have those qualities genetically. Naturally some people own these qualities, but if you really want to develop the qualities mentioned above, they can be developed. Many super successful people didn't have genetic possessions. Their backgrounds, environments, and even college education were not up to the mark. Despite all their disadvantages, they still reached the top levels because they were, and they are, ready for crucial change in their lives in all aspects. The top ten billionaires in America today started their journeys of success with nothing.

I know some of my friends who slogged strenuously to develop their business during the daytime, with a lot of effort. Compared to me, they strove a lot to add much to life, but their growth was very slow, even though they didn't want to reveal the reality. This was apparent from their behavior and life styles. The reason was that the same people did something contrasting at night, taking away by watching pornography, rather than growing and reconditioning their mental hygiene to prepare for the next day! One day I was trying to explain to my friend the consequences of what he did in his free time. But he reiterated that his mental health was so good that there was no need to take steps to keep his mental hygiene in place.

Many of us, every day, try to solve all our problems when we are unconscious with alcohol, or discussing things with cynics. Many of them see crocodiles in the water glass, as they live in uncertain fear and doubt. They think that the world outside is conspiring to rob them of their values. They wish to be more secure in life but remain insecure.

Super successful people and big dreamers cultivate different kinds of hobbies which are nourishing, advancing and make their lives an adventure, inspiring others to be happy and excited. Survivors never thrive. Their limited companies never grow unlimited. Don't delay to take your inventory on a daily basis, and figure out which way you are heading towards. All of us have the same time span in life, by which I mean the productive years of our biological age. It can vary, according to life style and life expectancy. I believe that the majority of people who are born in this world have talents within, but they don't reveal them on the surface of their lives.

Memory count

1. What do you represent in your life? Represent creative ideas and possibilities and make enough space in your imagination to dream big. When you dream, forget the current circumstances around you. What you are today is irrelevant; dream for the future.
2. Give life to your dreams, and believe that they are possible, feasible and achievable. There are no outlandish or impractical dreams that someone can pinpoint and show. You need to decide what kind of dreams you want to hold in your mind and work on them.
3. People who have written goals set realistic time periods to achieve those goals, and read them several times a day, as they have serious concerns about their dreams. They make them into reality faster than others, by magnetizing all the resources that are needed.

4. Personality can be changed, qualities are practicable, and skills are learnable. If you really want to be one among the successful, the possibility is still there. A majority of successful people are self made. Make up your mind and consistently work towards your dream.
5. Find out your true nature and gifts, and develop and apply them through hard work. You can transform yourself and others in the planet.
6. Focus, focus, focus. You will see amazing results. Concentrate on attaining fast and enough monetary values that enable you to move towards your other goals, whether-personal, financial or social.
7. Have fear of fear, for then faith will be established. It will motivate you to achieve any kind of goal. Maintain a pleasing personality. Monitor your attitude. Do mirror exercises and observe your facial expressions. Shape up your body, gestures and postures.
8. Don't stress about the nature of others or their mistakes. Try to study yourself. Honestly measure and review yourself. When you become a better person, other related things, like your surroundings, will become better and more comfortable for you.
9. Avoid negative thoughts about yourself. When you are down, go upwards with God. Never come to a conclusion about your life when you experience bitter things. Different methods lead to different results. Think differently, and rearrange your methods if they are not in the positive side now. Never say you are born to suffer.
10. Live life with art. Be different and do things in an exemplary way. Show others how great you are.
11. Many of us have the natural gift of charisma, which can draw others to our life, our business or to our organization. You can develop charisma through harnessing your characteristics.
12. Some people engage with their minds over a few minutes or hours to develop themselves, and the rest do so to undo and reverse their thoughts. Provide space in your mind to build you up as a prosperous and joyful being throughout the day. What you think, you will become, sooner or later. If your thoughts are strong, it will take less time; so make your thoughts strong.

"I close my eyes, then I drift away, into the magic night I softly say. A silent prayer, like dreamers do, then I fall asleep to dream my dreams of you."

Roy Orbison

All successful people, men and women, are big dreamers. They imagine what their future could be, ideal in every respect, and then they work every day toward their distant vision, that goal or purpose.

Brian Tracy

Dreams have only one owner at a time. That's why dreamers are lonely.

Erma Bombeck

We are all dreamers creating the next world, the next beautiful world for ourselves and for our children.

Yoko Ono

You were prepositioned on this planet. But you weren't predestined. A clarification of your life purpose will lead you to set your goals, achieve your dreams and reach your destination.

Keerthisinghe

5

Change Creates Characters

Suddenly one angel appeared before a wise person. Before the angel could speak to the wise man, the wise man opened his mouth. He asked the angel why he had come there and why he had brought two vessels. "I am not here to see anyone other than you," the Angel said. "I came to accompany some people. That is why the vessels are empty." The wise man thought it was a wonderful chance to go to heaven with his family. No need to make any effort! A free tour, he thought. But the wise man hid his desire within him as he wanted to test the angel. "How many people have you already found? If common people join you, I am not interested. I don't want to go as it will be beneath me." He, thus, revealed his ego.

The Angel said, "I came to you first. But there is one condition. You can't go like this." The man answered, "No, I will get ready properly." The Angel said, "Get ready to die first. Otherwise you will not be qualified." The wise man said, "What about all my things, money and property? I can't leave them right now."

The Angel said, "It's okay. If you can't die, you can't go to heaven quickly. But you can get into another vessel." The wise man asked, "Where is this heading to?" The Angel replied, "To success! Whatever you want, you will get."

"How much do I have to pay for the tickets?" the wise man queried.

"'No tickets; it's free of cost. But there is one condition. You have to change. Change yourself completely!" The wise man said, "I can't change, even if I were to die. This is me." The Angel was disappointed and he disappeared.

The moral of this story is that there are people on this planet who are not willing to transform themselves. They believe in their arrogant thought patterns and never emancipate themselves from the fetters of their dogmas.

The Counting agents were busy with their job. It seemed that it would take till the next evening to declare the results officially. I noticed that the agents, who had been appointed by me, were not happy while counting.

They had taken part in the counting of votes in the past elections, and they glanced at me with unhappiness in their eyes and facial expressions.

It was the 2005 presidential election, and we supported our party leader with the fullest expectations of a massive victory. Around 2 AM, I got a call from our party treasurer who had observed my great enthusiasm in the election. He thought that if we could win some electorates with bigger margins in my district, the electorate which I represented could be among them too.

"How is the situation in your counting?"

"We are trailing in my seat," I answered

"Is that so? I can't believe it," his voice softened.

"Ok, once it is finished, let me know," he said and kept down the phone.

Were we going to lose this election? Before the counting was over, I came to my election office, where many of our supporters were waiting to hear the happy news from me.

I said, "The situation is not good." A few hours went by and media channels started to declare unofficial results. The results of a few decisive constituencies revealed that we were definitely going to lose this election. For 11 years we had been in the opposition, and now again for another six years! I was talking to myself. Past trends showed that elected presidents would go on for two terms. Therefore, our party would be compelled to wait for another 12 years. The situation was quite disappointing and discouraging. Moreover, it was not easy to survive in the opposition as a mere party organizer without power. It required a surfeit of money and efforts to stay in the competition, especially in rural districts, where the government party threw many free things as bribes, in exchange of votes in the elections.

My conscious mind and heart were now struggling to solve something big. My rational intelligence forced my heart to eliminate all the emotions, worries, humiliation, and disappointment which were running through my heart at the moment. I couldn't control the emotions which had instantaneously taken control over me. I wanted to relax and free my mind of this huge setback. The dreams which we had built upon this victory were over. I felt that we had become victims, at a very young age, of our political careers. The only solution that came to my mind was going to a casino and playing to relax my mind. In fact, it was not my immaturity, but force of habit that dragged me there, whenever I was in a bad mood. One of the largest casinos in the country was on the road where my office was located in the capital city of Colombo. This was a bad habit that I had cultivated before I got into politics. Momentary relaxation became a habit. As I began to play at the casino, it destroyed my time, money, relationships and above all, my good consciousness. Whenever I played, my self-esteem plummeted, even if I won. I had acquired the bad habit consciously, and formed a habit that shaped me unconsciously.

I tell you, don't take it easy while performing certain acts. If your thought system is influenced by the very action which you want to do, it can easily turn into a habit in just a few weeks. If the habits that you are practicing are good, carry on, and hang on. They will advance you, enhance your capabilities and motor you to move to a space that you really want to be in, which will benefit you. But if they are anchoring your journey, you will stagnate. If you get stuck, there is hardly any escape, as it is very hard to quit. The reason is bad habits have teams and get on harmoniously with the similar kind of people. They will promote you, market you and brand you in negative ways.

One bad habit can connect you with many other bad things. When you play at the casino, consuming alcohol, smoking, untimely eating habits, killing time with no meaningful work, and inadequate sleep are a few examples. When you stop going to a casino, the habits which you picked up there, will not vanish. You have to struggle hard to come back to normal. Total rehabilitation is, hence, needed. There is a possibility of becoming a victim again because of other subsequent habits, which can drag you into the abyss if you are unable to eliminate all of them. I would suggest that it is better to cut the tree before the trunk hardens. Rather than sharpening your axe frequently, it is advisable to cut the tree down when it is weak and still immature.

Change is not easy. If we want to experience a real change in life by amending long term practiced habits and behavior, we have to carefully think about them and organize the reasons woven around it. Reasons should come from deep within the heart, mixed with emotions, so that the burning desire, like the fire from within, will compel you to move forward.

In the above incident, why did I change my habit of playing at the casino?

The answer is, "Because of my desire to enter into politics."

Why did I do so?

I realized that if I played at the casino after entering politics, people would think badly of me. Now it's crystal clear. I have realized my need and my reality.

I didn't have my own reasons earlier when I changed myself. I changed because of the influence of others and due to the perception of the society. My change didn't last for long, and habits emerged when emotions gained control over me.

I quit the bad habits, and now my addictions include reading, thinking, planning, and practicing, which help me to grow daily. Today I focus on character building instead of destroying the same. In a day, several times, I try to figure out how I can be a better person in every aspect of my life. I have given up all unhealthy addictions, including alcohol. The following are a few steps I took to improve myself:

1. I enquired from my heart about a clarification on my purpose of life on this planet.
2. I asked for a report about my intrinsic talents, which were untouched, and not transmuted into any value. I took an inventory of myself.
3. I asked for a detailed description of my future after 20 years; how it would look, what kind of wealth, relationships, health, and social contribution I would have at that time.
4. "What kind of skill should I learn to upgrade myself? How can I manage my time in order to be ready for the future? Will there be extra time to waste on addictions?" These were the questions that I asked myself.
5. I asked from my heart, "Are you willing to take challenges?"
6. I imagined how an addiction-free life would appear and felt a sense of joy from the heart, enjoying my will power.
7. I refused to consider others' requests or opinions on myself, regarding addictions.
8. I postponed temporarily the gratification for future benefits.

When you begin to change, people whom you entertained, and who benefited from you, will not let you do that easily. Their effect will be more powerful than your inner weaknesses. While my habits tried to overcome me from time to time, the above mentioned invaders also came along with modified options. "One beer in a day will be ok. Going to the casino once a week, and playing for small stakes, can cause no harm; what is life without enjoyment?" and the like. They little realized that I want to enjoy my life fully and abundantly for long. Not only for a short period!

Another thing which I learnt while I was trying to say no to my bad habits was that I have to give them up slowly. As a practice, I stop everything in a stern fashion suddenly, but start them again after giving myself excuses. This time I started slowly, and gradually my bad habits disappeared. This gave me a greater understanding.

I couldn't escape my negative circle quickly; though I managed to avoid them slowly and they avoided me very fast.

I understand that life will not move toward progress without firm and positive changes. If you refuse to change your mind, no words will change, no actions will be initiated and no results produced. It is our responsibility to change situations, instead of allowing situations to challenge us.

In order to undertake some radical steps for a change in society, stop waiting for someone to take the initiative. We have to go forward positively; we can't wait for others. We can only wait for ourselves.

Progress is impossible without change, and those who cannot change their minds cannot change anything. If all those people who are hopeless and helpless only turn hopeful, it will bring about a change in all areas of their life; finance, lifestyle, and relations.

We can change many things easily, such as our hair, looks or appearance, face, house, spouse, city, country, name and address. Will it be as easy to change our character? Not at all! It is a hard task, and one that many will not do inwardly. Change involves development and maturity that most don't want to see within. The education system cannot visualize it, nor can money or rules. If you really want to, you will do it. When you really need to progress, it will involve a change of mind, and a change in your thought patterns. What do you think? Do you have positive thought patterns in all departments of your life? If your thoughts are negative and not elevating you towards any development, then you have to identify them and eliminate them swiftly. Do consume good mental supplements that enhance your energy levels. Through affirmations, prayers and goal readings, you can supplement your mental food.

Also, strive to monitor your inner dialogue. Don't let the little man come out from your heart with negative proposals, based on your past bitter experiences and observations. Don't allow him to underestimate you, without judging and measuring what you are today. The best mental supplement that exists within your reach is having unlimited scope. That is imagination. You can travel through your future while undergoing a mental change in your current conditions, to attain the expected higher levels.

To see real change in your life, you have to begin some activities which you are not following at the moment. Many of us do not concern ourselves with our mental hygiene. Take action to recondition your mind, eradicate negative thoughts and instill positive things instead. Increase those activities which give you positive results and make your life productive. If you read one book a year, try to read at least one book a month; not just read, but try to assimilate the ideas that stimulate you to upgrade yourself, and read again and again to apply them. If you want to become a published author and write one page a day in your new book, try to write three pages in a day. If you spend five minutes on your mind work in a day, do it at least for fifteen minutes with prayers, affirmations and goal readings. If you listen to motivational messages sometimes, you could do it every day as a habit. There are many interesting videos available in YouTube that cover all areas of life. If you attend motivating seminars or conferences, you have to do so often.

Some habits or activities need to be brought down. If you consume alcohol two-three days a week, cut it down to once a week; if you eat large meals, cut down on carbohydrates, and take some good organic food supplements. There are very good proteins, vitamins and minerals in the direct selling market made from plant nutrition. If you sleep eight to ten hours a day, cut it down to four to six hours. Some behaviors have to be removed permanently. If you meet friends who give negative opinions when you share something, or are cynical, stop hanging around with them. It will be difficult to do it at once, but you have to do so for the enhancement of your future.

A powerful imagination can change lives and work as a changing agent. The past and the present will not contribute anything to change, as only the imagination of the future does. It activates the creative faculty of the mind, offering you the key to an open future. If you lose that key, you will miss the future.

Situations or circumstances cannot be changed. But we can change ourselves. But many don't understand that in simple day to day life. Outwardly we do; when winter comes, we wear winter clothes. Likewise, when obstacles come in your journey to achieve something, your mind refuses to change the cause for good, unlike winners do.

What I understood was that I should look differently at the material and moral values in others whom I can easily impact around me; my family, relatives, and friends. I have to reflect the change in my character, so that they believe in me, looking at me as a leader who follows and manifests important laws of leadership. Why do we respect and believe in our God? He showed us miraculous change. He influenced us. He changed death into resurrection. Why do we respect our fathers; because they bettered our lives in many ways; feeding, nurturing, and showing us moral ethical values? How did one person become the Father of the nation in the country? He changed himself and influenced the whole nation to change. Many changed their lives from slavery to liberty.

Many people believe that time will change everything. They validate procrastination by giving excuses. They say wait, be patient, be calm, but being patient will not change anything. The country won't change, and the economy won't. If you are in the doldrums, the opportunity will slip and pass you, keeping you unchanged because you are neutral. Don't wait for others. Your friends, relatives and loved ones can't change something crucial in your personal life. They can motivate you, but you have to change by yourself, if you really want to feel happy, and achieve abundance in your life. In all areas of your life, you are the one who has to reflect the change representing ideas and possibilities.

If you are one among the few, aspiring to change the society and world, you must believe you are the one who can initiate and influence whole segments, by offering a radical and revolutionary impact. There are myriad examples; despite being in a wheel chair, Theodore Roswell did. Churchill did, Mahatma Gandhi did, and Mother Teresa did, despite obstructions. If you care and strongly believe, and are ready to be a river and not the reservoir, you will empower others and become empowered before you build your empire.

Feeling is most vital. What do you feel about yourself? Are you happy? Can you give a value for your life? What kind of reputation do you carry for yourself in your mind? Are you fulfilled? The way you think, the words that you speak, the actions that you take; do these give you a good feeling at the end of the day? Do you have a feeling of guilt? What do you think about your personal life? What kind of words do you use while having conversations with your spouse, children, loved ones or servants? Do you feel good about them or feel that you shouldn't have talked in a certain way? Do you feel good or guilty about your actions? If you have guilt within yourself, it will cause low self-esteem. You have to change all the patterns by using force.

How do you feel about your professional life? Can you really be happy about what you do and your performance? Do you feel sometimes, "I should not have done that?" Are you just doing your work mundanely, or are you performing through maximizing your capabilities to deliver excellence? Are you misusing your time gossiping and criticizing people, blaming others? After having fun, engaging with social media sites during work, what do you feel at the end of the day? Do you think that you have ample self-esteem?

How is your spiritual life? What kind of feeling do you have? Are you happy about your spiritual maturity? Are you spending life adding Godlike features? In short, do you have a high level of self esteem, unlike a petty kind of pride?

Memory count

1. Find the purpose of your life and resolve to make the necessary changes to become what you want to be. If you are not clear about the purpose of your life, the change that is to be made also will not be clear.
2. Overall change is essential if the current condition is not advancing you towards your goals. If you don't change the cause, the effect will be the same.

   If current results are not good or are close to underperforming, think about the beginning of the process, discover the cause, and change it in the next attempt. Get different results, necessary to change the cause. The cause can be your thought or an action.

   Thought patterns, words, actions have to be changed. Positive mental attitudes will lead you toward dramatic change. Change inwardly and outwardly, mentally and physically. Inward renewals bring outward reforms. Travel into your inner journey to see and value the things which are stored there through your mental eye. If they are not compatible with your growth and developments, correct them, shaping them through mental vaccinations. Scientific prayers, positive affirmations and reading the goals that you have already written, will aid in getting subjective mind attention to deliver things you expected on the surface.

   Change your physical condition if it is not up to the mark. A big belly will make you slow and lazy. It will cause pain in the legs and take away the mood to work energetically.

3. Apply the change in your personality to show drastic improvements in your personal, professional and spiritual life. Let others notice them at first glance, and share your new changes with your well wishers. Their praise and appreciation will uplift you to be courageous enough to stick with new changes. When you read more and listen to motivational speeches, your knowledge in different fields will sky rocket and the level of your confidence will increase.
4. Change should be a true transformation, and not a temporary pretense that causes more harm, leading to a low level of self-esteem and respect. Determine to undergo major changes, and always begin with small manageable tasks. Don't try to take a U turn to amaze or impress someone, as you can't maintain that for long.
5. In order to make a change in any field, be it your character, income, life style or relations, you need to make a commitment. A committed person has a good relationship with God. People lacking commitment are not capable enough to achieve anything laudable and big in life.
6. Commitment should be protected through determination and self-discipline. No man can maintain commitment without self-discipline. Successful people are disciplined in all manners.
7. Why should you change? Don't take the opinions of amateurs; listen to the voice that comes from within your heart. The heart is your spiritual temple. Professional advice may help you too.
8. Focus on the ultimate results, which will bring you rewards. Don't focus on how tough it is to change. The process of change will not be easy. It is uncomfortable and painful to take a decision and change the mind in the beginning, but be clear about the decision or choice you have made, based on what you want to be. Focus on your future shape. You will get the will power to do so.
9. Introduce new and novel patterns into your life, which aid you to form habits, systems and routines in your life to rebrand your life. Convince yourself by taking actions. When you make a habit, you unconsciously impress your subconscious mind, and those impressions, in turn, make subconscious convictions. If they represent the positive side, then the result will be for your highest good.
10. Reading, listening and attending seminars and conferences also are good mental supplements that boost your immune system to fight temptation, which comes, from time to time, to take your dreams away.

11. Trust the results of positive imagination and envision all the areas of your life after applying these new changes. Entertain happy feelings until they attract and embrace you.
12. Apply pressure on yourself to make deadlines to change or begin something; otherwise, you will remain comfortable in your routines and systems. The more complacent you become, the more distractions will appear.

If you do not change direction, you may end up where you are heading.

Lao Tzu

Never believe that a few caring people can't change the world. For, indeed, that's all who ever have.

Margaret Mead

Change will not come if we wait for some other person or some other time. We are the ones we've been waiting for. We are the change that we seek.

Barack Obama

You must be the change you wish to see in the world.

Mahatma Gandhi

When we are no longer able to change a situation, we are challenged to change ourselves.

Viktor E. Frankl

Change is the law of life. And those who look only to the past or present are certain to miss the future.

John F. Kennedy

6

Best investment is investing in you

Work while you have the light.

Henry Frederic Amiel

Rejection by you brings about the most harmful and irrevocable mental congestion. Once it is established within our thought system, it remains not just a congestion, but turns into a mental trauma. It can neutralize you and freeze all your active nerves. Just imagine you are stuck in traffic for hours; what kind of uneasiness do you experience? There is no way out as your brakes are on. You can't move, and sometimes, other drivers keep honking. Irritating, isn't it?

You feel like getting out and running away. In the same way, when you reject yourself, again and again, you will feel you want to give up, hide or quit, or run away; sometimes you feel like saying bye to your own life. It happened to me.

When I was badly broke, having lost everything I had, mainly the name I had built and the fame I had got, I rejected myself totally. I said to myself, "You stupid man, you don't know how to manage anything, and you don't have tolerance. Why have you kicked away your fortune? You can't take firm decisions, you have ruined yourself, and there seems no way out! Go to hell."

In those days, I started my days surrounded by the pain of rejection. I couldn't see my face in the mirror, as I would get angry. I developed thoughts based on my bad experiences and observations, and the things I underwent. I always rejected myself, and had nobody to stand up on my behalf. No one accepted me, because I had programmed myself to being rejected by everybody and anything touched by me. I blocked my avenues, and didn't notice the opportunities under my feet. I perceived them as great evils that stood before me to eat up my body, associated with things and the people whom I had regarded as unworthy when I was in clear consciousness. The reason was that I felt unworthy and incapable of raising my head again. I truly believed my given time was over.

Many of us fear rejection when we try to initiate, present or sell something, an idea, a proposal, a service or a product. What I understood was based on my own experiences. People who fear rejection reject themselves in their minds, and convince themselves to believe in that rejection before they physically meet it.

In fact, it is because of your expectation based on the self rejection concept. When you go for an interview or a one on one meeting, your vocal cords collapse, your tongue stumbles and fumbles. Before anybody rejects you in the society or the market, you have already rejected yourself.

How I overcame this disastrous and unfortunate mental condition:

1. I resolved to avoid people who compared me unfairly with other friends who were better off than me.

   Though I wished the best to everyone, I didn't want to feel ashamed of myself over comparisons. I didn't have a competition with anyone except myself, even if others didn't realize that I had to go that extra mile to reach my goals and uplift my self esteem.

2. I trained my mind to understand adversity as a university. It is not an easy task to recondition the mental store, eliminating long term deeply-rooted thought patterns. Many habitual thoughts in the process evolved into habits. I chose to change myself, build my character and began to concentrate on ultimate achievements, instead of the difficulties that I underwent, or was undergoing, on my journey. Previously, most of the time, I had focused on my obstacles and problems, which had always pulled me down. When those things happened, being human, it was hard to accept them as strengthening forces, but those adversities were like universities. You learned many things, not only academic, but also extra activities to try your abilities, along with a gamut of avenues to develop and become a better human being. People, who have fully utilized their time in universities, may understand this.

   I learned many things because of my adversities, which I couldn't have otherwise learned in a lifetime. It was more like a University. In a University we study in one faculty at a time. On the other hand, Adversity teaches you many things, almost as if you studied in different faculties within the same University.

To understand the nature of the disaster, you have to go through it psychically; in universal experiences, you can't experience that rigorous state of the difficulties. When you are in the midst of great disaster, even your loved ones, friends and society will react in unexpected ways. It is not easy to find measures to rise up again and all these are big challenges.

I experienced the same; survival became a major issue, especially when I shifted to foreign lands.

3. I relaxed my age barrier. I don't accept my body age, even if I am unable to reach my targets as planned. There are many living examples of people who have achieved success at different ages. You have to be healthy and maintain your fitness. This is possible at a low cost.

   As soon as I got the financial capability to afford the best supplements in the world, I did stick to them. I didn't bother to celebrate my birthdays. I still don't! I consider my birthday to be on the day I attain remarkable and huge success. Achieving optimal health is a big challenge and also a choice of the people. While everybody ages and dies, healthy aging could always be a choice. It is helpful to enjoy your success and not to be a burden to your children, loved ones and the socicty in your old days.

4. I tried to notice something that was remarkable within me.

   Teachability was the great gift which was hidden in me. If I didn't possess this, I wouldn't have had the guts to fight back, because all my material resources had been used up. Moral and ethical literacy are values which can't be converted to money, but also the most useful blessings for the journey of future success. Generosity was considered as my foolishness. But I liked that quality which aided me to experience a feeling of gratification always. It uplifted my self esteem amazingly, which helped me to stand still in any situation.

5. I tried to find someone superior to me and all human beings. I held onto my faith and built my self confidence based on Him.

   Why did I want to believe in someone superior to me? When I was broke, and low in self confidence, in order to bounce back, I needed some sort of great help or divine support. There was nobody to tell me things, and from whom I could expect energy beyond the limit.

At one time, I was like Superman among relatives and friends, all of whom were settled with their limited resources, even though they wanted to extend help to me when it was needed.

6. I used to think that world had the right to see my colors one day. The world banked on new versions of capital, arts, books, architecture, infrastructure, voices and the like. I felt that I could be one of those or more.
7. I decided to invest in me. To build myself, improve, develop, reshape, transform my life and apply myself to the world. I could be an application that could remodel and regenerate energies in others' lives. I could create new forms of skills that could be reproduced and copied to donate maximum output to this world.

Story

A King had three Princes. When they were sent away for education to a far away state, the King told them before they left, "Remember there is some wealth beyond this kingdom!" The Princes retained that seriously in their minds. When they were grown, they neglected learning valuable skills which were to be learnt to rule the country. Instead, they thought always about how to acquire the enormous wealth which their father had mentioned. The King got to know that they were not learning properly and refused to hand over the power to them.

The Princes thought of expelling the King from power so that they could inherit the kingdom and wealth.

They conspired carefully and made a tunnel to enter the King's bedroom without attracting the attention of his security. They procured sophisticated arms which the King didn't possess. They were able to capture the king and they forced him to tell them about the wealth which was of more value than his kingdom.

The King laughed, and said, "It's already in you. You are creative, you did team work, hard work, smart work, and you have mastered them for a bad cause. If you master them for moral and ethical causes, you would be unstoppable and capable of invading and conquering the entire world." Now the King was ready to hand over the kingdom, but they refused unanimously. The Princes realized the truth and went back to complete their studies and learn more skills.

The Moral of the story is: People are looking for something greater outside without noticing the things within them.

Do you have the right qualities within you? If so, you have to enhance them. Otherwise, you have to acquire them. When you decide to take charge of yourself, you have to charge your battery, to be able to act with confidence. If your battery is too low, you will have very low confidence to make the calls, because you will never know when it will get over. After establishing due confidence, you can implement your comprehensive on board plan. Before starting the efforts, you should realize that the thing you are going to do is tough, not easy, because you are going to achieve something big. Big achievers face big challenges, fail greatly and achieve greatly; while taking action, fear will appear before you in many forms; fear of 'no', fear of 'can't', fear of rejection, and when they appear, you can't run away. You have to overcome them.

How can you do that? Regardless of how big they are, you have to bring forth your burning day to day and long time needs before them, and let them fight the external fear and internal needs. If you have a concrete base of your organized resources, they will supply the back power to overcome fear. You can empower your internal resources first, which will help you to organize your external resources. Internal resources can be strengthened by changing your attitudes through mind works, prayers and affirmations, and external resources can be strengthened through adapting new skills, making new relationships. When your dream stands in front of fear as a huge giant, it will disappear in a moment. Thus, begins the process of achievement. But don't think that it will not come again; you have to vaccinate yourself to get immune to chase it away when it attacks. Super successful people know these techniques and they apply them when necessary.

When I decided to drive my dream firmly, I sketched my daily routine parallel with my goals. I made a time table accordingly. I selected books related to motivational and inspirational stories, to get insights, ideas and useful guidelines for my business. Setting aside a few hours for reading, I went through YouTube and found some professional motivational speakers and trainers. I listened to them again and again. Every time I listened to the same clip, I found something different and clicked new things to be added in the scripts which I was writing for my speaking career. I would practice for a few minutes, speaking aloud some parts of my scripts.

Recently I found something missing in the time table. I had not allocated time for thinking; most of the time I had to think, and be away from external distractions to organize facts for my book. But the most difficult thing was to stay away from others. I had to guide my only employee, whom I hired as a trainee, for marketing purposes.

I find now that, rather than reading newspapers and watching news channels and TV debates that consume many hours in a day, it is more useful to learn something new, and master and create an asset which can be transmuted into huge finance and residual kind of monetary equivalents.

Investing in self is the most important investment, more than any sort of available investments in the world. Many don't bother because it doesn't provide instant material rewards. If you want to create something extraordinary in life, while engaging your income generation activity, you can initiate it. I have more free time in a day because I am unemployed. I scheduled to work eleven hours initially, and I soon got tired and I couldn't do that. It's been two months since I started my new mission to write my book and become a professional motivational speaker. Many distractions appear and, most of the time, I am behind the schedule. But still I can be happy that I have started to move forward. I write at least one or two pages of my book every day and do some reading, speaking and listening practices. I am improving and stretching in different areas which will aid to turn me into a valuable product.

'The more you uplift your personal value, the more your net worth goes up.'

Keerthisinghe

Memory Count

1. Don't reject yourself. Many people do this to themselves after setbacks, disappointments and failures in life. They come to conclusions about their incapability which is harmful to future progress. If you accept that you are not suitable or qualified to achieve something big, who else will think that you deserve to be someone? Focus on your plus side and qualities that can add value to your personality.
2. Be aware about your true potentialities. Make a vow to yourself that you are going to test your talents and gifts 100%, and leave this world a better place because you lived in it.
3. Practice until you get the competency, and sustain this in particular fields. Routine activities are necessary. Practice repetition and be persistent. Ultimately, the activity becomes part of your life, and according to the quality of excellence, monetary values will be added on.

4. Learn from your experiences to avoid repetition of mistakes, but don't live in the past. Plan your future from your future. Erase all unpleasant memories and never let them come to the surface again.
5. Organize as many resources internally and externally as possible. The more resources you have, the more options there appear in every aspect. More is better. More mental power energized through mind works, optimal health, myriad contacts and healthy relationships, more than one income source, skills and training in different areas - all these possess high price tags. In other words, I would say, fill your vats with the best wine.
6. If you invest in yourself, you can develop 'you' as a well crafted product and obtain a better demand in the market. Don't stop investing in yourself once you have acquired some paper or professional qualifications. Many give up and focus on mere survival after a stage. Focus on maximum production, productivity and creativity for your success.
7. Don't disregard the most powerful and good stimuli that keep you in fire; love and sex. Maintain them throughout life in an acceptable way. Focus on optimal health and keep your physical and mental health at peak levels.
8. Inaction leads lots of rejections. Do concentrate on proper action as it will get you accepted everywhere. When it is needed to demand, do it. When it is necessary to go fast, do so. When it is time to re-shape, do it. When it is time to be listened to, do it. Appropriate action will avoid unexpected rejection.
9. You have to be the commander of your life; don't let fate, destiny, or luck control your life. You are not a gazette's notification signed by an authorized signatory; you are the creation of a master craftsman and He never made puppets. The control buttons are in your jacket; control your life. There is nothing out of control in your failure or success. Even if something does happen due to unavoidable circumstances, there is always the possibility to regain your life.
10. Never encourage yourself to retire without getting utmost gratification. Don't worry about your age according to your birth certificate. Feel good with exemplary reports of mental and physical health. Don't affirm that you don't have a good memory, or that you feel weak in the

morning. Repeat to yourself always that you are ready to take any risk for a good cause.

11. Don't believe in something just because others do; even in the case of your parents, spouses, relatives or friends. Sometimes they may not be in a position to stand with you. If you build something in you, that is the best, as nobody can steal it. If you are smart, it can be transmuted to your passive income and create enormous wealth.
12. Affirm that you are creative and capable of handling anything that challenges you. Believe that wonders can happen in your life. Affirmations are a very powerful mode of mind exercise that convinces your creative faculty.

You have to be constantly reinventing yourself and investing in the future.

Reid Hoffman

I think the number one safe haven where people put their money is to invest in yourself first.

Hill Harper

If you look to lead, invest at least 40% of your time managing yourself - your ethics, character, principles, purpose, motivation, and conduct. Invest at least 30% managing those with authority over you, and 15% in managing your peers.

Dee Hock

My philosophy is whatever you do, you've got to invest in yourself. If you don't, there are a lot of people out there who will get the job because they're more prepared than you.

Karl Urban

Take the time to shop for yourself and cook. All of this is an investment in yourself, and if you're not going to invest time and money in what you put in your body, then what are you going to spend money on? It's kind of the most important thing.

Joe Bastianich

7

Fear, no more

If you know the enemy and know yourself you need not fear the results of a hundred battles.

Sun Tzu

The simple definition that has been given in the English dictionary for fear: An unpleasant emotion caused by the belief that someone or something is dangerous, likely to cause pain, or a threat.

Though the definition is simple, the result that generates from fear is very harmful. It makes you a victim of the system, and brings down your self esteem. You will begin to disrespect yourself, and feel unworthy. Fear will slow down your productivity, shrink your capabilities, engender doubts, cause you to miss opportunities and make you settle for little things; less money, a small house, an average job, a poor lifestyle, and unwanted relationships.

It was 1990 when I was in my advance level class for the University entrance in my school. I had a major crush on my classmate. She was beautiful and stunning. I had neither the words to express how beautiful she was, nor the courage to express my love, due to the fear of rejection. I thought too much. What would happen if she said 'No'? Would she tell others? What would others think about me? Would they laugh at me? And so on!

At last I decided to write her a letter. I was adept at *Sinhalese* literature and good in poetic language. I beautifully decorated that letter, praising her pretty features. It took a considerable time to finish, and at the end, I was amazingly confident of winning her heart after giving it to her. But my biggest problem was to hand over that letter to her. I spent many days, keeping the letter in my pocket. I smiled and talked with her more than before; I put my hand into my pocket to take the letter out to give it to her, but I couldn't. Sometimes I felt that she liked me enough for me to give her the letter. But fear controlled my nerves and prevented me from taking further bold steps.

An idea came to my mind. I could assign someone to hand over the letter. One of my friends, who studied in the same class, appeared to be the most suitable person for the errand. He was bold, talked with everyone and made jokes, especially with the girls. In fact, he was a mischievous character, with a tendency to fight with people. I chose him and he happily agreed to the mission. I expressed my fear and he consoled me by saying that he would look after any problem that could arise. He added if she didn't like the letter, he would force her to give it back. I trusted him fully and I asked him not to open and read the letter. He agreed.

Days faded away. Every time I asked my friend what was happening, he would ask me to wait for some time. After one week, I again asked him about the results, and he said it would take more time. I observed her behavior, and couldn't notice any difference.

One evening, when I was going home, I saw a couple in love, walking by; they were holding hands and laughing. When I came close to them, my heart beat went up drastically. It was them. My friend and the girl whom I was in love with! My friend gave me a casual wave and the girl smiled at me. I tried to smile back but my lips were stiff. I couldn't lift up my hand to wave to him.

The next day, I asked my so-called friend about what had happened. "How dare you walk with my girl, holding her hand?" He chuckled and said, "My friend, your letter was beautifully written. I rewrote it and put my name and gave it to her. It worked."

"How could you do that?"

He said, "You missed your chance because you hesitated to hand over the letter by yourself. Why should I have missed the chance, without opening it? I opened it without any fear. I know your writing skill and so I rewrote it and gave to her. Next time, try to act by yourself; don't be afraid." I controlled my impulse to smash his face. But he had taught me a lesson, even though I had lost an opportunity. The wonderful thing was he believed in my skill, when I myself didn't.

Once I was given an opportunity to give a speech in a very reputed University in India. I was happy because it was the start of my career. In fact, my maiden speech! On the other hand, I was apprehensive. Fear came to the surface and held down my leg. Because I was going to speak to the faculty staff, most of them were professors and PhD holders, and I didn't even hold a master's degree. Inside me, a little voice came and said, "You shouldn't do it. You don't have the experience. You will be stuck. You know these intellectual guys are not easy. They will ask you some questions using technical words and terms. You have never given a speech in English. I advise you to take more time. You are not up to the mark." This was my little man; he was always like this. Don't do, must not do, don't go, don't sign! This was his style. He had discouraged me on many occasions in my life. This time I was not going to listen to him. I began to monitor my inner voice.

This time, the big man came in. He said, "Time is running out; don't waste it; take this opportunity. It will be a showcase for you. You are a great speaker. You have given speeches in your language before. English you can brush up, and once you have rendered five or six speeches, you will be fine." I closed my eyes. Something was being revealed from my creative intelligence. My synthetic faculty didn't have the power to solve this.

I discovered that, within me, I have creative intelligence in my subconscious mind. I lodged my complaint on it, and in a few minutes, an idea struck my mind.

Go to a website and find the photos of the staff of the faculty to whom you are going to speak. Print the photos and paste them in your wall and give them a speech. Assume that they are earnestly paying attention to you, amazed by your speech. When you see them in reality, you will recognize them very well and there won't be any anxiety. You can be friendly with them. Even if they ask questions, it's not necessary to answer all of the questions separately. First, listen to all the questions and give a common answer.

I stood up. Would my legs tremble when I got on to the stage; would my tongue stumble and fumble over my words? No, no, no. Don't worry, and remember you are organizing your knowledge and going to intelligently direct it. You have a practical plan to build your speaking business as a career. You have to set goals, and you will not settle as an average speaker, as you were not rated so before. Whatever you have done in the past, you have done in the best way possible. Prepare yourself. The more you practice, the more confident you will turn. Just imagine the crowd is expecting your arrival on the stage, eager to listen to you. They give you a great welcome. A round of applause! You get more motivation to speak and words flow endlessly as you perform beyond your limits. Most importantly, have the courage to be on fire. If you have a big fire within you, you can emit good heat; remember you are not alone. Your creator, Almighty God is always with you.

Normal fear is acceptable to take the necessary measures to protect ourselves from danger. But abnormal fear is ruthless, and brings along with it many unfortunate events. We fear many things that could happen to us in the future, but 99% of these things may never happen.

We should have fear in God, for then we will have fear of sin to do immoral things.

According to Lord Buddha, we should have 'shame and fear'. In Pāḷi (Language), 'hiri-ottappa: means "moral shame and moral dread". When we lose shame and fear, we are unable to differentiate the human from the animal, because animals don't have shame and fear. These two factors govern all actions of mankind.

It is obvious that people fear rejection, which they have to face on numerous occasions in life. Dating and marriage proposals, job interviews, in sales and marketing products or services and so on.

Fear of failure is also a common mental state that prevents us from making a move when we are about to strive for something. What will happen if I fail; what will others think? People will laugh and make up stories. This fear causes many talented people to live mediocre lives. Many fear success. What will happen if I achieve great success? How will I handle it? Many people never get success due to this fear, and even when they do so, they end up broke. Many lottery winners have faced this unfortunate situation, as they couldn't handle their fortunes due to fear, and have panicked and ended up in bankruptcy.

Thinking will not overcome fear but action will.

W. Clement Stone

We can easily forgive a child who is afraid of the dark; the real tragedy of life is when men are afraid of the light.

Plato

Only when we are no longer afraid do we begin to live.

Dorothy Thompson

True success is overcoming the fear of being unsuccessful.

Paul Sweeney

Have no fear of perfection - you'll never reach it.

Salvador Dali

8

Have courage to fail and the spirit to win

"It's fine to celebrate success but it is more important to heed the lessons of failure."

Bill Gates

Recently when I was in a relaxed mental state, I asked a question to myself. How many times have you failed in your life? Earlier I had convinced myself, boasting to my colleagues that I had experienced many failures in my past. Was that really true?

My heart answered, "Yes, you failed, but not during all the times you considered as failures; only two times. I was a little confused. What made my inner person answer so confidently? I had assumed that my failures had started since my childhood.I was not born with pain, but as I grew up, I began to experience many hardships and pains in my life. When I was eight years old, my father passed away in the blossom of his youth, at the age of 37; my mother was 30 and never married again. My brother was five and my sister was three. I was the only one who had a clear memory of my father, and who experienced clearly his demise with shocking pain at that time. My father was a businessman with a good reputation, about to begin his political career at the time of his death. All our dreams were shattered. He wanted to move us to one of the metropolitan cities, planning to get us admitted in city schools. My mother was a primary school teacher and she didn't have enough business knowledge to manage my father's business, and our economic situation became tight, day by day.

I lost my pillar, my mentor; my father had English knowledge even though he didn't possess a college degree. We completely lost that flair. My mother couldn't speak English properly, and was unable to create an English speaking environment at home. Today, that is why I emphasize on the importance of English education, as, due to the lack of the knowledge of English, on many occasions, opportunities slipped away from me, and I couldn't grab them and move forward.

Thus, my city school education evaded me, and I had to study in rural colleges, where I got few opportunities to sharpen my skills and inborn talents.

I had a dream to become a cricketer, but because the school where I studied wasn't equipped with proper training and coaching facilities, I lost that dream too. The entire scope of my future changed due to my father's death.

I considered this misfortune as a failure.

Today, I understand that this incident, and the series of problems we underwent, was based on different circumstances. We can't change those facts. Those were roadblocks that stymied our plans of success. Those situations occurred, not due to my action or inaction, but entirely due to external and unexpected factors.

I understand today, the show is not over. Life is like a movie theater, which has many shows. When one is over, another show starts. Circumstances come and go. Coming attractions will play. Sometimes, even though the next one is a horror movie, drama, or thriller, we have to wait patiently until the show starts. Life is also like that; we have to hang on until the day comes in our favor, while being confronted with all the circumstances and situations, whether we like it or not.

My mother struggled a lot. I could remember her getting up at 4.00 am in the morning to prepare food for all, including my father's parents, sisters and brothers. Without electricity or a gas connection those days, she had to cook on firewood. Wonder what motivated her to make that effort? Having three children and being a single parent, she couldn't afford much, as it was tough even to afford education for us. She underwent three major operations in her abdomen. In spite of all that, she didn't give up her efforts to give a proper education to us and somehow, she managed to get admissions for my brother and sister in popular city schools. When I was in the university, I felt that a big responsibility was on my shoulders. I had to work part time. I tried to do many things to cover my expenses and finally bought a house for my mum. We left our ancestors' house due to internal family disputes.

My first business venture was in the advertising business. Up to date I had considered it as one of my failures. But my heart questioned me and asked, "Did you give enough time to develop that business? Did you gain new skills in the process of your business? Did you implement new methods and techniques? Did you change your attitude to make it successful? Did you take effort and time to make new and valuable relationships? The answer is 'No!' So you neither started that business properly, nor made sufficient business applications to uplift it. I can't say you failed. You quit that business due to an unsuccessful performance."

Failure is an excuse for losers to hide from life and the same failure is an energy booster for winners to transform their lives.

Keerthisinghe

Those days I was hungry for money. My heart always told me, "Hey, you have to do something soon; you have to look after your mother, oversee your brother's future and your sister's education and marriage." These alarms had become my responsibilities and my passions.

Again I started the property business, brokering, to find buyers. With no investment in hand, I didn't follow any business principles or fundamentals to run it in a successful manner. I had only burning needs and desires, along with an overweening desire to become rich. Again my efforts were not enough; I failed to persevere that far. I didn't have any goals to achieve as I hadn't set any.

Today I realize I could have striven more to enhance my talents to achieve success. My needs were not fulfilled; my mother's home, and the like! My inability and all these failures kept triggering me from time and again.

My third business attempt was a travel agency in the hospitality industry. Once again, I started from scratch, but I took 100% responsibility this time. I took huge risks and challenges, and practiced and implemented new methods. My efforts paid off and my wealth creation process started. Within three years, I owned seven vehicles, including luxury jeeps and cars, two houses, land, and tolerably good savings in the bank. I travelled to many countries, attended to business exhibitions, bought a house for my mother, sent my brother to Japan, arranged a nice marriage ceremony for my sister at Hilton hotel, helped my friends and enjoyed life until business broke down again. Recently, I understood that I had a tendency to enjoy my life more than I deserve, and to procrastinate without focusing on long term perspectives.

It was a real failure. My heart confirmed that I ran that business for five years, associating with negative people, practicing unhealthy habits and making hasty decisions, and in the middle, diversion of focus and priority were the major reasons for my failure.

While I was running the travel business, I grabbed another opportunity which was one of my dreams. I entered politics.

I used my creativity when I was in the university. I founded a party for students, got involved in student movements and led it to victory in the second year, defeating the long established victory of another party. When I got into party politics also, I did the same and got the highest preferential votes, defeating the experienced candidates and members who were in the office.

Even after that significant victory, my party had fewer members than the ruling party and we became the opposition party of the provincial council. In addition to my office, I wore many hats – that of an organizer of a big constituency, media secretary, member of debate panels on television, member of the economic affairs committee of the national body of the party and a member of the national youth front.

I used my talents passionately. I spent 150 million rupees for the election campaign and other welfare activities in my district, money which I had earned from my travel business. I spent much money for the presidential election which was contested by my party leader, but it was unsuccessful. Four years I was in office and my financial condition went down drastically. Based on the ideology which I had on national issues, I decided to support the then president, and took a break from active politics. While I was in politics, I made decisive decisions, and delivered the goods to my people. Investing my time and money, I built my personality and reputation, which turned out to be one of the assets in my comeback. Though I considered my decision to enter into politics as a great failure, it aided me to get great success in future. It further reminded me of my mistakes and thus, I learned many valuable lessons. Therefore, those failures became solid foundations to success.

On 5 June 2008, I went to Japan and started a car export business with my Japanese friend. However, due to some audit issues in his company, he couldn't fulfill the requirements of my visa and make arrangements for a long stay business visa for me. It was, indeed, a real tragedy and completely blocked my way to go further. My heart couldn't accept it as a failure.

I chose India as the next place to regain my wealth and soon started a hotel accommodation business without a penny in hand. However, I was able to sign a contract with a hotel owner to rent his hotel for 3,50,000 Indian rupees monthly, and managed to earn a considerable amount of money, which helped to enhance my life style. It was an experience of a new trade and clients. My major clients were Sri Lankan groups who came on pilgrimage tours. I enjoyed opening a sari boutique inside that hotel where I gave accommodation to people. Despite various envious acts committed by the previous hotel management, and people who had made hotel reservations a business, I did a wonderful job that opened the eyes of all.

Unfortunately, swine flu began to spread in India and the Government of Sri Lanka prevented pilgrims from traveling to India. It was a full stop for my business. This was an unavoidable circumstance. I gained new experience, and changed my attitude in the process of achieving that goal. I became a stronger and wiser person, even though I had had lost a business opportunity. I understood that people, even my near and dear ones, assumed that I was a failure and thought I wouldn't be able to raise my head again.

"Don't let the noise of others' opinions drown out your own inner voice and most important is to have the courage to follow your heart and intuition."

Steve Jobs

I couldn't follow that opinion. I decided to go to Europe. Previously I had traveled to Italy, France, UK and Germany. So I could manage to go to Italy. My ultimate intention was to go to UK, settle there and begin a new life. But in less than a month, I managed to join a consultation firm in Italy owned by Sri Lankans, that offered various kinds of services related to stay permits and family visas.We found a new way to expedite the procedures of taking family visas, but when that led to some legal complications, we were compelled to stop the business, after losing quite a bit of money.

Again I was pushed to the wall with financial hardships making my life uneasy. I neither got material rewards, nor considerable mastery from this attempt. I realized that I had taken an unprofitable risk while doing that project, with no patience shown, no research or study, just a mistake, which could not even be considered a failure.

I completed two years in Italy and raised a question within myself several times, having talked to my heart. I paid careful attention and my subconscious mind advised me, "Go back to India. You will find something remarkable. It is the only place where you can get success." The only thing which I knew about India was that it was a country with a developing market. We had the potential to grow if we really wanted to do so. Yes, that was the place where you could come across major opportunities.

It was never an easy task to move from one country to another, and to settle with the situation. While I was in the same place or less, I noticed crucial changes had been happening in India, and its people within a short time. Close friends had told me that I had made a huge mistake in leaving India. If I were in India, I could have achieved something bigger. I need not have worried anymore as all the chapters in life had left unforgettable memories and lessons.

A new chapter began in India. When I came to India, my weight was 86kg, which was not comfortable, and one of my friends introduced me to a person who dealt with health supplements. I needed to lose weight and get my earlier shape back.

I followed his instructions and within 6–8 weeks, the result was tremendously good as I lost 12 kg. I was impressed. He invited me to attend a meeting to see the business plan of the company. It was direct selling business. He introduced me to two guys who had achieved enormous success in this business in many countries, including India.

I sensed the plan was lucrative, ethical and practical. This business could be introduced as multilevel marketing, or as direct selling. It could be done with minimal investment. The concept was enlightening, and while building your business, you could help others. It attracted me as this could bring me in contact with many people. Never an isolated character, I loved to talk with people and share my knowledge, and learn about their experience and culture, through socializing and networking.

I started to study to understand this networking business as a subject, and read several books, including The New York Times' best seller, 'Rich Dad and Poor Dad', written by Robert Kiyosaki. I thoroughly went through sales and marketing plans. I was fortunate to meet several top achievers in this business, as well as many foreigners who had succeeded in making huge teams and revenues. I even met the second generation of some business owners.

But this time, I needed to avoid mistakes as much as possible, especially the ones which I had made on previous occasions. So, in order to have a deeper knowledge of this business, I attended many meetings and seminars, to gain more knowledge of almost all the products. Even today I use many products that are result oriented, economical and eco friendly. I learned how to do demos, conduct one on one meetings showing sales and marketing plan to prospects. I went to Thailand to attend a big rally. By now I was convinced that financial freedom, hope, a glowing future, residual income, being with loved ones, fame, health, looking good and young, helping people - these were the things I needed.

I jumped into business and started to prospect people. As was my habit, I dressed smartly. I began to enjoy meeting different kinds of people. I believed that we could respect people and also earn respect from them by wearing clean and neat clothes while meeting them.

Even though I was a foreigner, my contact book was filled with so many new contacts and prospects that connecting with people was easy for me, but the greatest challenge was fixing appointments for the meetings. Everyone was busy in their own worlds. I yearned to explain this amazing opportunity, but many were satisfied with their salaries and living in an unstretchable world. Many accepted the concept as very good and feasible, and were satisfied with the products. Many more admitted that they needed to have a second source of income, but they were short of time.

It was time to develop my character and habits. I became more punctual, unselfish, learned how to overcome fear and rejection, practiced patience, changed my attitude, improved my communication and management skills, acquired leadership qualities. I also learned how to handle finance, team work, value people's efforts and understood the importance of perseverance.

For two years, even though I didn't invent a new wheel, I added creative methods and techniques to this business, making reasonable efforts to build my business with this platform passionately. Being a foreigner facing many challenges in communication and getting along with people, I achieved some levels, until the company was forced to remove all foreigners, including me, due to government rules. But I still believe this concept is a workable and one of the best ways to acquire wealth and a residual income, if you make efforts without any diversion or distraction for at least five to ten years. You may feel it's quite a long time to persist, dealing directly with people facing so many challenges and rejections. Of course, the results you get will be amazing, leading to a complete transformation of you.

My heart clearly noted this was a great failure, but I gained great mastery. Even though I was unable to continue in this business, I garnered a lot of knowledge. It was like going through one of my higher education centers, business school, and practical MBA.

I understood that even though I lost many battles, I also found new ways with new arms to fight the war. Having missed many kicks and tries, I again applied different techniques in the game, and faced failures, one after another. The match was still not over; even if it was over, a new series would come along in the journey of life.

My heart finally encouraged me, saying, "You are capable of doing more things than you have ever imagined. You will find the right goals. The road might be rough and tough, but always target high level goals and pursue them with integrity; be ready to overcome the challenges in a more creative way. The planet is waiting to welcome your contribution."

My spirit started to flow as I got the encouragement to strengthen myself. Like the eagle soars high above the sky, the almighty God makes the righteous man prosper in His time. I was reminded of what the prophet Isaiah says about this, "Though he stumbles seven times He will raise him up seven more times."

Memory Count

1. Have the courage to think clearly and allow your heart to speak before you. Set foot on your desired ground. It doesn't mean that you have to be cautious, and research and analyze things for a long period without having the guts to initiate. You have to approach your dream with scientific formulas that have been presented by successful people with proven techniques. Don't consider just opinions.
2. Measure the values, talents, skills and abilities you possess and discover how much they can help if you apply them to your determined task. If they match with what you are doing, they will multiply production.
3. Don't get into something that doesn't make you happy or sharpen your talents. It means that you are not able to use your gifts. If you are compelled to do something for survival, do it. But don't turn into dead wood, sticking to that indefinitely, leaving your goals behind until it becomes your whole life, limiting your potentialities and compromising your dreams.
4. When you do something that you love to do, unconsciously, your talents will be released to excel the outcome, and resources will miraculously appear to complete that task. Then you will be magnetized, drawing the attention of others.
5. Give a considerable time period for your task and try to find out innovative ways to get maximum results. If you are underperforming, add some creative plans. Get some new training to upgrade your knowledge and skills. Find some finely crafted human resources that add value to your organization.

6. Find your role model mentors and coaches. They are the navigators who will direct your path in any field to get success. Determine to be the most sought after in the field to get fullest attention, leading to returns and rewards.
7. Discipline yourself. "A man without discipline is like a ship without an anchor." Discipline will push you towards persistence, enabling you to reach your desired destination with élan. If you can make actions discipline yourself, persistence will align itself with it.
8. Don't eat the desserts before the main course. Delay your gratification until you get the expected accomplishments. It doesn't mean that you have to be so stingy as to not even offer coffee at a business meeting. But don't go to Las Vegas to play at the casino using your credits.
9. Expect barriers, fears and failures, but look upon failures as mere delays of your ultimate achievement and not defeats. When you accept failure as defeat, you dig your own grave. Repeat to yourself every single day, "I am born to rise".
10. Be optimistic and don't lose your enthusiasm in the mire of misfortune. Focus on your results, and not the difficult journey you undergo. Always imagine a happy ending.
11. Focus on your abundance willingly and let wonders shine through the law of attraction.
12. Develop your character and practice some characteristics that enhance your talents; be punctual and unselfish.

Thus, it is impossible to live without failing at something, unless you live so cautiously that you might as well not have lived at all, in which case you have failed by default.

J. K. Rowling

"Sometimes by losing a battle you find a new way to win the war."

Donald J. Trump

9

I am Hungry

For me, life is continuously being hungry. The meaning of life is not simply to exist, to survive, but to move ahead, to go up, to achieve, to conquer.

Arnold Schwarzenegger

When we were small, we looked forward to school holidays. They gave us exciting, memorable moments, like going to my mother's paternal house. Both my parents had large families. Twelve members in each family! We had more than ten-twelve cousins of the same age or with little difference in ages. All my cousins would get together and play. Sometimes our uncles also joined us. It was a real thrill. Sometimes we did adventurous things when we strayed away from our mother's attention.

Another reason to go there had to do with the business. My father was a businessman. I was considered as a child with a businesslike mind. One time I saw a lot of chilies piled up in my grandma's house. In those days, vendors came by van and buy them. Unnoticed by anyone, I went to the road, stopped the vans and brought them home. In fact, we were not allowed to go to the main road. It was the first rule I broke, and the second was to talk and keep company with strangers. Sometimes in our area, children were kidnapped.

I took the risk because I was hungry for money. When grandma was able to sell something, she gave me some money. But this had gone beyond the limits. My father was incensed and I was given a stern warning. He sent them back without selling anything. Thereafter, whenever my father was around, I would avoid my business activities.

One day I noticed some vendors had come to purchase betel nuts from my grandma's house. She cultivated betel nuts and she had a very fertile harvest. Vendors who came to our doorstep bought them at a very cheap price. I presented a small business plan to grandma and she agreed. I said I would sell them in the village fair and that she had to pay me for it. It was a big change; all the betel nuts were sold. My new nickname was 'small merchant'. When our school started, I always wore new clothes and had enough money in hand, to treat my friends at the school canteen. Even for my small needs, I was hungry.

As I grew up, my hunger grew along with me. Those days I was hungry for small things; today, I'm hungry for big things.

On one vacation, we went to our mother's sister's house. While we were hanging around in our village, I noticed a person making something outside his house. I inquired from my cousin brother who said he was making very good herbal oil which enhanced the growth of hair. Suddenly something clicked in my mind. My aunties from my father's side had very long hair, and those days, they were worried about the health of their hair. I approached that man and asked him the price. Then I informed my aunties who were happy and ordered the oil. I made quite a good profit, of course.

One day, I was waiting for an auto rickshaw to go to Ambience mall, Gurgaon. The sun enjoyed showering the maximum energy that it could show in that season. It was not easy to bear the unkind sun rays. I stopped one auto guy and asked him the fare to my destination. "A hundred and twenty," he said. I got angry and I shooed him away.

After about five minutes another auto came and stopped beside me. I asked him the fare and he asked for one hundred. Again I refused.

After some minutes, another auto came, and I asked the same question and he said eighty.

I asked about five-six autos. No one agreed to my price, which was seventy rupees. It was not easy to do this exercise standing in the sunlight. Another auto hurtled into sight, blasting loud Hindi music. The driver smiled at me and asked where I wanted to go. I mentioned Ambience mall and asked him how much I had to pay. He asked me how much I could give. I said seventy. He said ok.

When I was on the way to the mall, I tried to understand the difference among these guys. This guy was hungry; he wanted to earn money with passion. His strategy was right, and so he was not going to lose. I observed his auto. It was clean, the music was on, and while driving, he was also humming the song; he was enjoying what he did. He asked, "Sir, do you go out every day?" I said, "Yes!" He took my number, "I will come and pick you up!" he said. He had some sort of vision because he was hungry. Others wanted customers. This guy was hungry for customers. I asked him, "Can you go inside the mall premises?" He said, "Why not?" Most auto drivers were scared to go inside because of the security people. He was enthusiastic. "Why?" My mind said, "He is hungry." I finally handed him eighty rupees because I liked his attitude. He said, "Thank you, sir!" and hurried away.

Next day I called him again. He answered the phone promptly and came on time. I introduced him to my friends also. I noticed he bought a new auto after a few months. He was on the way to achieving his goals. Until we bought our own car, I used to go out with him.

My hair dresser, Kabir, who worked at one of the best saloon brands in Ambience mall, also had similar characteristics. Armed with a bright smile, he wore clean clothes and was polite. He provided excellent service, and carefully and patiently dressed my hair. Once a month, I colored my hair, and he would take care of my hair like his hair. He even supervised its washing. After cutting and hair color, he offered a free face clean up and tried to negotiate with the manager to give me a discounted rate for a foot massage. One day he told me that his dream was to open his own salon. He was hungry. He cultivated good relationships with clients for the future. He was not surviving for today, but planning for tomorrow. I liked this nature always and encouraged him, saying, "You can do it." I always gave him good tips. One day I got a call from him. 'Sir, I have opened my new salon.' Now I am his regular customer in his own salon.

Memory count

1. Enjoy thrills in your life like a small child; children get excited over small things which keep their enthusiasm alive.
2. Love this world and your life. Your positive attitude creates positive moves.
3. Do something significant and amaze everyone. Don't make it a habit to only get amazed by things done by others and call them geniuses. You also can do wonderful things, if you really want to.
4. Do something more than you are paid for. When you add value to your product or service, the satisfaction that you offer will increase in volume with repeated customers. If you are an employee, the individual brand value will be established among others; if it is an organization, good will will grow.
5. Be opportunity conscious. Seek, research, stretch and restructure constantly; seekers are the creators.
6. Break those rules that limit you. Some people believe in certain myths. Based on that, they make rules that limit. "Our family will not allow it";

"It's not good for our caste or community." "How can I sell?" These are familiar complaints.

It is not up to me whether I win or lose. Ultimately, this might not be my day. And it is that philosophy towards sports, something that I really truly live by. I am emotional. I want to win. I am hungry. I am a competitor. I have that fire. But deep down, I truly enjoy the art of competing so much more than the result.

Apolo Ohno

We're all caught up in circumstances, and we're all good and evil. When you're really hungry, for instance, you'll do anything to survive. I think the most evil thing - well, maybe that's too strong - but certainly a very evil thing is judgment, the sin of ignorance.

Anthony Hopkins

10

Settle with Devils

Rumors spread everywhere in the village that a devil would come soon and eat them up. Except for one wise man, all the others ran away to survive. The wise man had had a very good education and enjoyed a good status. Everybody respected him. He thought, "Let the devil come! I will settle with him."

The Devil came and he was surprised. He found only the wise man and his family. The wise man talked to him diplomatically and said, "We can talk and settle the matter. You don't need to eat us." The devil agreed.

For the first three months, the devil ate all his cattle, and the man was left with no milk to feed his family. He asked his family to tighten their seat belts because this was a serious situation. They did so. Within the next three months, the devil ate up all the horses and the man's transportation business collapsed. He said to his family, "We have to face this situation!" and they had to tolerate it. Over the next few days, he survived, selling the hope that he would bring back some village people who had run away. He cleverly convinced some people who were hidden somewhere, and brought them back, and the devil ate them up. Finally at the end of his tether, he asked the devil to leave and the devil ate him and his family up.

The moral of this story is that today, many people try to settle within their comfort zones which gives them temporarily relief. Ultimately they become victims of the same comfort.

Today many people settle, contented with their living conditions. They are contented with half measures, merely satisfied with their jobs or small traditional businesses, because they can survive paying day to day bills. Many never try to upgrade their skills, and settle in their jobs until they get the experience or find a similar kind of job with a small pay hike. When they age, they get some minor promotions and small pay hikes.

When their children want to go for higher education, they wait until they get selected to government universities, as they don't have the money to give them a technical or career based education. If they have provisions, they settle for third grade institutions which have no name and value in the market. I have met many individuals in India who have MBA degrees, but work in retail outlets as sales guys. The reason is that their qualifications are not properly recognized as they have not done their education from a reputed college.

When medical issues arise, many people settle with minimum facilities, sometimes placing their family members in a dilemma. When you don't have sufficient money to give medical facilities to your loved ones, you settle with your mind and say that's life.

Most of the time they ask their children to settle in arranged marriages because they want them to do so. But their children don't. They settle with devils on many occasions. But parents aver that their children are well settled. Recently one lady doctor committed suicide in India because she found that her husband was a homosexual.

Many people suffer from this 'settling' disease. First they settle with their minds, reveal their attitude to family members, colleagues in the work place or fellow members in society, and influence them to be like them. They are contagious.

I am not against people who work for their livelihood. But I am worried that people settle, by merely working for someone and mortgage their dreams, just for day to day survival. They sacrifice their dreams, and do not realize their full potential and talents. Many people come into this world and go out, unnoticed.

A Middle Eastern proverb says, when you are born, you cry, and the world rejoices; you should live a life in such a manner that when you die, you rejoice, and the world cries.

I do not suggest that anyone reading this book should have a simple and settled lifestyle. Instead I encourage them to have a fulfilling life style. Live life to its fullest. To be simple at heart is appreciated. Contribute something valuable and memorable, not only to your loved ones, but also to the society. The world has the right to see or hear something from you, and experience the things you have achieved on this planet.

Imagine if great inventors and scientists, who had had major breakthroughs, had settled in their comfort zones! Would we be able to communicate quickly, travel comfortably, live extravagantly, work productively or cure diseases miraculously?

What would have happened if dictionaries were not written, and great artists had given up their endeavors on the way, settling with mediocre mental states? If John C. Maxwell had not written 'The Leadership Bible', I would still be the follower of my destiny.

Many people settle because they don't believe that they themselves can do something extraordinary. They expect to get work done from someone else. They often claim, "I am done; it's not me, not my cup of tea." They suffer from low self esteem, and remain cornered with settlements which they don't deserve, even though they think they deserve them.

Some people think it is wise to be careful, not realizing that everything is changing. Knowledge is being updated, and humans are being replaced by machines. Major business trends are swallowing small enterprises. Industries are restructuring. Companies are downsizing. Are you still settling with what you have? Or do you want to find something more like plan B or plan C?

Many successful people have plans B and C. It's not because they are not confident of what they do. They believe in putting their eggs in different baskets. If plan A fails or they underperform, they have plan B in hand. It is necessary to have financial freedom and a continuous flow of income. More than an active income, it is vital to have a passive kind of income which offers you royalty.

When I had my travel company, I neglected my career as a lawyer. I deliberately postponed focus on another source of income generation. Instead of wealth creation, I diverted my attention to politics, inventing a way to pump my money into a river. I had an active income source. When the company was liberated from my grip, it started to go down. I was broke. If I had had a source of passive income, I could have continued without experiencing bankruptcy. Unfortunately I had settled solely with my active income source.

Reasons why people settle

1. Attitude

   Thinking style, the way one sees things

   One of my aunties always used to say, "I don't want my children to catch the stars. It is enough if they get some teaching appointments in government schools and settle." See how an attitude influences people. Her children tried to become teachers. One succeeded and one did not. But they never thought of doing something else. Their mindset was settled and restricted. In such cases, it is rare that some people emerge, practicing an independent thinking style.

Many face danger in aiming too low because they never look ahead. They don't have a vision, as they are wanderers. Some people can see and envision, but they don't want to do so by themselves, always preferring to follow someone else.

2. See only through eyes

   People see and believe in what they see. Most of the time, they judge accordingly. They have a close, short sighted focus. They always look for something to settle, unable to see anything beyond their eye sight. They have no idea about their mental eye, or their subconscious mind and the creative intelligence within. They should tap into their subconscious mind and know what else they own.

3. Will power

   Some people believe only in hard work, and depend on will power, unable to combine this with doing smart work. Smart work doesn't interpret as crooked work or using others to work for you. It only means you are capable of using universal experience, rather than experiencing your own mistakes and failures, repeatedly. There is immense literature which has been written, and workshops and seminars that you can attend to get some insights, to avoid many mistakes which people commit generally when they climb up their ladder of success.

4. Resources

   Many concentrate on what they don't have - money, investment, staff, or infrastructure. They are unaware that they have to initiate something with a burning desire, not with just ordinary desire, so that the opportunity will not slip away and resources will follow.

5. Talents

   Many think that they don't have any talents or skill. Or they think that they have only one talent, but that's not entirely true. Everybody possesses various talents and gifts. Believe me, you have more than one. Let your heart speak up and clarify that, to give a chance to your hidden talents. Try something whole heartedly; don't try half heartedly, keeping your desires somewhere else. Unknown talents will appear and shine if you initiate and act on your breakthrough goals.

Generally people talk about someone who is doing good or is well settled in his affairs. In order to do significant things in life, you have to value excellence and not settle in being average. People who have contributed amazing things to this planet never settled for small things. Have a passion for big things, think and dream big, and start small; that's how some people shine among the stars today, in any arena - politics, films, arts, music, business, relationships, and social contributions. That is how people are trying to explore Mars. You will be among the stars if you start something with burning passion. Cry for the things which you don't see yet, for unacquainted things; it's your vision.

Take life as a real kick. Don't let your past kick you away from the goal. Kick out your past and drive your future. Don't wait for someone. People will say sometimes, "You can count on me." Don't hand over your dreams to someone and don't appoint caretakers for the same. You have to protect your dream, and passionately follow it by taking some risks for a good cause. Risk who you are today. Sacrifice who you are today and have a passion to transform yourself into a worthy character, making some unique marks so as to be different among ordinary players.

Memory count

1. If the wave is downwards, don't try to swim upwards, and against it. It's not persistence. Go with the wave, find the stronghold, and then start again and persevere in your task. Have normal fear, as it's healthy and alleviate abnormal fear.
2. Settlement is not a winner's quality. It's the fake satisfaction of a loser. Settlement is contagious, and if you set an example of settlement, the next generation will follow you. Don't settle with devils.
3. Believe that you deserve something extraordinary. Your faith will aid you to receive it.
4. The world is in rapid change; react to it. Don't be a victim of technology. Use it effectively.
5. Focus on wealth creation for the future, instead of income generation for today. In your lifetime, you can create wealth that can pass down to the next generation, but the income which you generate using your physical efforts will not. It will stop once you stop your labor. Create future returns that give you enormous wealth with multiplication.
6. Don't wait to see with your eyes and believe in unacquainted things; let wonders happen. If you see a majority of people who make a living, and take living examples for your guidance, you will miss the big picture because you believe in what you see. Don't hesitate to expand your

level of eagerness to receive avalanches of abundance through the magic working powers in life.

7. Trust merely in hard work is not advisable; do some smart work and expect some miracles.
8. It is wiser to step into second base, while keeping one foot on the first. Have options in life which are better and safer. Be risk oriented, though always for a legitimate cause.
9. Never miss opportunities. When they appear, don't think of the missing infrastructure. Think of the results beyond obstacles.
10. Never say it's not me, or it's not for me. If everyone says this, what will happen? Strive over a considerable period for novel and strange opportunities to appear. If you have passion you can make the impossible, possible.
11. Determine to do some important tasks without further delay. Treat them as an emergency. Don't let your needs die inside your pocket.
12. Refrain from asking your family to settle with things, and develop the ability and character to get maximum rewards and enjoy the fruits. Life's not worth living unless you enjoy the fullest happiness with your family, because they are the most important shareholders of your life.

A dream is your creative vision for your life in the future. You must break out of your current comfort zone and become comfortable with the unfamiliar and the unknown.

Denis Waitley

Life begins at the end of your comfort zone.

Neale Donald Walsch

Move out of your comfort zone. You can only grow if you are willing to feel awkward and uncomfortable when you try something new.

Brian Tracy

People tend to play in their comfort zone, so the best things are achieved in a state of surprise, actually.

Brian Eno

I've been out of my comfort zone a lot, and it makes me more vulnerable, but I have to draw the line somewhere, and don't think I would go skydiving!

Hannah Storm

11

If you can do it once

If we were to rub two pieces of wood together, but stop and attend to something else before sparks were produced. We could never obtain fire.

Traditional Buddhist teaching

When I was in Italy, I used monthly season tickets to travel in metros and trains all the time. I used to dress well and people used to give me respect calling me Avvocato. Avvocato means 'advocate' in Italian. Advocates are respected in Italy. My house owner specially made my restroom, installing new amenities to give respect to Avvocato.

I had quite a big house with four rooms rented in Novara city. Every day I went from there to my workplace in Milan. Apart from me, there were four people who stayed, and two never contributed anything as rent. It was quite expensive because we lived in the centre of Novara city.

One guy who lived with us was always trying to get close to me and showed more loyalty to me than others. We had dinner together most of the time, and enough wine was there every day. Everybody used to bring something in the evening, and wine was on our priority list. Singing, while drinking, was the usual thing. Even though we underwent many hardships, the darkness at the end of the day brought us some kind of relief.

One day I didn't have money to buy the season ticket. I didn't even have money to buy two tickets to go to Milan and come back. My friend always inquired about each and every simple matter from me. I didn't know why! Maybe it was out of curiosity or habit. Sometimes he irritated me.

He noticed that I didn't have money for tickets. He had never bought train tickets in his life. Many commuters don't buy tickets; you can notice, in every train station and metro station, how the metro staff catches people and writes fines. He said, "Don't worry. See my tickets." He used tickets that he had used before. He knew how to erase the dates punched by the ticket machines, using a chemical which we used for cleaning toilets. He would erase the date and punch it again. Most of the time, he succeeded. Sometimes he got fined, but never paid. He had another system for the metro. He used old tickets torn into two, and used them in old machines which were installed next to the ticket counter. It worked.

He arranged tickets for me. They were not new, but used ones. I followed his instructions. I was very nervous. I passed the entry in the same manner and came back in the evening. Next day, I had money, but my friend said, "Come, don't worry! Use this again. You buy me a packet of cigarettes. Don't waste the money on tickets hereafter." I did that several times and it became the norm.

IF YOU DO IT ONCE, YOU CAN DO IT AGAIN.

We are more vulnerable to bad things than the good things in our life. It is easy to learn and become perfect. When we do bad things we lose our moral values, and when we do good things, we develop our character and maintain our ethics. If we hang on and persevere, results will be generated. You will form habits and habits will form you. I regretted what I had done before, and today, I applied the same theory for my personal development, my pushups, my physical and my mental work.

Recently I started doing ten pushups in a day, and then increased the number, day by day. I started reading one chapter of a book a day, and I started watching one motivational speech a day. Thus, I moved on and made smooth progress.

Persistence is very important in success.

Excellence is a true art. It can be gained through proper training. When a particular act becomes habitual action, you will discover the rhythm in it. If you want to be someone, you have to repeatedly do the required activity until it becomes your habit. When you have a habit which you believe in, and when you perform it excellently, others will start to believe in you. Just imagine a great singer. When he comes to perform at a show, before getting on to the stage, people believe that he is going to do an amazing job and they wait for that. That belief has been established through the excellence that he has gained through perseverance. Even though it comes in one song or one show in one night, behind the curtain, perseverance is laid down.

If you want to achieve something great in your life, it can't be done in one night. Even though you have amazing strength, you will not be able to do so. But it can surely be done through perseverance. If you don't quit, and keep doing it until you see the final expected result, it can be done. It's not the strength which you possess; it is the strength which you acquire through perseverance, continued over a considerable period. It depends on how fast you learn or master new skills. Anyway, it can never be a short period in any field. Specializing in a particular subject or its mastery will give you value, and that value can generate money and fortune, beyond just the skill of doing something to survive or doing something as a hobby.

If you learn something, you acquire knowledge.
When you assimilate something, you get comprehension.
When you plan properly, you will organize it, and
When you apply your knowledge, you experience it.
If you start something you will be excited, and
When you practice it, you will be confident.
If you persevere you will be energized,
And when you have patience you will be disciplined.
At last when you achieve your dream you will be magnetized.

Memory count

1. Have the courage to take the first step. Human beings are created and designed to take steps and moving forward is natural. Once we are born, we begin to move and gradually take steps. Remaining frozen and in the doldrums is not a normal and acceptable condition. Besides, if all of us are bogged down and neutral, what and who will move in this planet?
2. Resolve to take the first step from your conscious mind in all vital departments in your life. Think and shape yourself in all aspects. By moving forward, what changes will you bring to your life and the people who are around you? If that move helps to nurture yourself and others, adding moral values to uplift your brand, don't over research, but measure the possible consequences. People who analyze things rigorously have starting trouble, as they always see the disadvantages of the event.
3. If you want to write a book, set a goal and make a dead line, before you start to write. If you can write one paragraph on the very first day, you will be able to write a new chapter in your life. Believe me, that is how I began to write this book, progressing day by day. Facts galvanized my mind as my creative faculty gave me the guidance to organize the ingredients; that's the power of motoring. Don't anchor yourself and cry for the bank accounts of others. I may not have been a great writer in the beginning. But average people, who want to enhance their lives, always become action oriented, turning great in the process. A great

many ideas evolve in people's minds, but they can't see them in material form, because they have not yet initiated the process. Remember to initiate something that gives enormous results. You need a strong will, coupled with a burning and compelling desire.

4. You are doing a job and are not an executive having a million dollar package. You need to be free from bosses and enjoy financial freedom. What do you do? If you have good perks to survive in your comfort zone, you will lack the motivation to shift from your current conditions, and you will merely engage with your job. You will never find time to take actions for change, and all the opportunities that loom before you will seem like devils. Don't wait for retirement to begin new ventures; many people retire from their lives when they retire. Wasting the active energy in your youth is not advisable. Start working part time, and give two hours to your venture. If you can't physically be involved, delegate some professionals. When you start something new, your mind will start shifting slowly, causing your body to take the actions that are necessary.

5. Learn from the process. Don't wait to turn into an expert before starting something. If you are a product, you sell yourself and your unique talents. While selling in the market, you get a perspective of the real shape that fulfills gaps in the needs of customers.

   In order to become a famous speaker, you need to talk in public, make mistakes and, thus, learn how you can give memorable messages in effective ways to the audience. Even if you practice for years, writing scripts, practicing before the mirror, or in a room alone, will not help. Take actions to initiate, and repetition will follow.

6. You need to get married to someone again after your divorce. Hanging around at popular meet ups for divorcees, and sharing your bitter experiences with people in the same boat, will not serve the purpose. Erase and stop sharing past history, be optimistic about second chances, and move forward to search for your dream partner. You will find your choice.

7. Flatten your big belly to get rid of your ill health, and start healthy habits. If you can go for a walk one day, and cut down the intake of carbs and sugar deliberately, you can do it again. Try the best supplements in the direct selling market. Doing things again and again, even if they are simple actions, can be immensely beneficial.

8. Have a long term perspective. Don't find short cuts and easy avenues to reach your destination. I did, and it didn't work out. Five year, ten year, twenty year plans make you disciplined enough to persist. Long terms are not for procrastination. Whatever work you do right now should be impeccable and convincing.
9. Start small but well, one job at one time. If you try to feed your baby with too many things at the same time, the baby will start crying. Treat your new venture like your baby. You can make her a little uncomfortable, but don't make her cry.
10. Energy levels do not remain high all the time. When you feel high spirited in mind and body, do something more, instead of wasting that energy for low value or no value tasks. Remember to repeat and make constant efforts.
11. Do not consider low results as excuses to quit; they are reasons that guide you to make attempts again and again. Repeat them until you achieve excellence.12. Don't repeat or continue mistakes. Once is enough. Twice is more than enough. Your third try should be right in the goal and in the game, not out of the goal and game.

Great works are performed not by strength but by perseverance.

Samuel Johnson

Permanence, perseverance and persistence in spite of all obstacles, discouragements, and impossibilities: It is this that in all things, distinguishes the strong soul from the weak.

Thomas Carlyle

Perseverance, secret of all triumphs

Victor Hugo

Perseverance is a great element of success. If you only knock long enough and loud enough at the gate, you are sure to wake up somebody.

Henry Wadsworth Longfellow

12

Life is tough; never look back

The Lord shall preserve your going out and your coming in from this time forth, and even forevermore.

Psalm121:8

Many a time, life brings forth what it likes to manifest; events which we don't like to reflect on. Sometimes we name it fate or destiny. These have power too. In fact, you empower them unconsciously. They turn into life and then life takes control of you. When that happens, you will be framed, your abilities and talents cornered, as you misuse them or you don't use them to the fullest. Life moves on while you're stuck with your circumstances and situations. When problems show up, you will feel there's no way out, and run as long as possible, only to notice that they are still chasing you.

Some friends, co-workers, or people who are in the same business, field or profession, overtake you and you look at them and call it their luck or chance. Absolutely wrong! Do you think that people who have won in their lives have never been confronted with the enemy called problems? Of course they have been and they still face them. The difference between a loser and winner is that a loser trembles and flees when problems come into the picture, and a winner waits to meet them and hammers them into solutions.

What life does to us:

Life creates hard times, keeps you bogged down sometimes, and brings worries, regrets and disappointments.

It puts you down, fails you, and makes you feel hopeless and devastated.

It keeps you on hold, and can make you neutral. It makes you angry and ashamed. When you solve one problem, ten appear on the surface.

What should we do to overcome this overwhelming problem?

Toughen your nature, nurture your personality, and don't see things from too close, but view them from a distance. A close dimension of a problem can never reveal its solution. Focus on your desired destination, and you will see the problem stand next to you like your slave, working on your commands. Have the courage to command your problems and never let them override your rules. What are your rules? Your rules are the vision codes you made, envisioned by yourself to walk towards your journey of success.

Life can use emotions, thoughts, words, people to discourage you and send you back into your own shell. You can't escape from this attack unless you take control over yourself. When life beats you and embarrasses you, always get an 'A'. Pass and don't settle for a 'B'.

When I was studying for my university entrance exam, my mother sent me to her brother. He is a teacher and still gives tuition for economics. There I learned two lessons; economics and life. The lesson of life was harder than that of economics.

He was a well built man with tough rules. He taught enthusiastically and made every effort to teach his students to get excellent results. I was an average student among his favourite bright students in the class. I was very playful, and most of the time, my attention strayed away from his lectures. One day he asked a question of me and I couldn't answer. He came to me and gave an unforgettable A grade shot to my back.More than the pain, I was embarrassed, as everybody laughed loudly. He went back to the stage and declared that after the examination results were out, he wouldn't be able to conduct his class in this city because of me. He predicted that I would not pass in his subject, which would bring him much embarrassment. Even though I was angry with him, I had to come back home with him on his motor cycle. On the way, he stopped and bought ice cream for us and said, "I will continue lobbing shots at you till you get an 'A' in my subject!" and he chuckled. explained his own hardships during his schooldays and how he reached this stage with minimal facilities. He explained that many people wanted to relax, waiting for luck which never arrived. This resonated in my mind all the time. After a few months, the examination was held and the results came after three months, with only one 'A' pass in his class. It was me. Today he is one of my favorite uncles.

When I was in the university, I worked part time in a TV station as the presenter of an Art program. One day, while I was preparing for the recording, the chairman of the network came to the studio and complimented me, "You have got an excellent voice. Why don't you join the NEWS Telecast?" I just smiled and he said, "Go and meet the person who is the head of the news unit." The next day, I made an appointment with the head of the news telecast and went and met him. He got my screen test done and said, "You have a very wonderful voice, one which even I don't have!"

I went out from his office with the big hope of joining NEWS telecast. But I was never called for News. I was crestfallen when I noticed that the brother of the head of the news telecast department appeared in the news telecast later.

People will treat you in differently even when you are the most suitable person for a particular opportunity. People will promise that they will join you, help you, invest in your project, but in most cases, they will disappoint you. Have the courage to follow your dream because it's yours. When you allow your creative faculty to keep you updated with new ideas, innovative ways and fresh paths to approach your dream, you will not be isolated, even if everybody leaves you in an adverse situation. Humans have the amazing power to overpower any adversity and turn it into their advantage and benefit.

When I was actively involved in politics, and an assembly member, my party selected me as a member of the TV debate panel. Very few got this opportunity. I was a regular on the TV those days along with parliamentarians who represented the other parties. One day I went to the National TV channel, where the other members present there represented a similar kind of ideology. I did my job well, and at the end of the first round, during the break, one person said to me, "I thought that your party would send a big guy with better knowledge than you about this issue." And they all chuckled. I instantly realized he had made this statement to put me down, to mentally discourage me and get an advantage in the next round. I countered him, saying, "I cant see any thing small I have when compared to you guys! Do you see it?" They kept quiet.

Life is a song - sing it. Life is a game - play it. Life is a challenge - meet it. Life is a dream - realize it. Life is a sacrifice - offer it. Life is love - enjoy it.

Sai Baba

Life will embarrass you

There was a time when I was a very regular customer of Costa coffee in MGF Mega city mall. Every morning at 10 o' clock, I used to report there like I report to my office. I met my prospective clients over there most of the time, because the networking company which I associated with was located in the same building.

Sometimes I had more than three meetings in a day, though it was rare that I conducted all the meetings which I fixed in a day. Many didn't show up. That was the nature of this business, and moreover, the nature of unsuccessful people. The staff at Costa coffee were friendly because I never sat there without buying something every day. I spent at least five hundred rupees on the things I usually purchased - two coffees and a muffin. Many thought that I was quite rich, but yes, not in my pocket, but in my heart.

One day I ordered coffee and offered it to my prospects, hoping that I would receive some money from my part time dealing. Unfortunately it didn't click. I waited until evening, embarrassed to tell the Costa coffee staff that I was not in position to pay. In fact, on previous occasions, I had reminded them about my bill and paid it. It hurt my feelings, but this was life.

Unable to pay the bill, I went home and that whole night, it stayed in my mind. It took four days to receive my money. After that I paid them back. They didn't mention anything, but I suffered. That's called life.

Life isn't about finding yourself. Life is about creating yourself.

George Bernard Shaw

The truth is you don't know what is going to happen tomorrow. Life is a crazy ride, and nothing is guaranteed.

Eminem

You have to expect and encounter attacks and challenges on your life's journey. If you feel that they block your path, that's a misconception. They are blessings that come in disguise to strengthen your level of confidence. When you confront them, your unstoppable creativity will come to the surface with better solutions.

First you have to undo fate and destiny from your mobile dictionary. Don't keep them even in the trash, but completely eliminate them, for only then you can encounter your situations effectively.

Encounter situations, and develop yourself. In order to do so, chalk out routines and systems, not for a day, a week or a month, but for throughout your life until you go to the grave. In this process, you will empower the real you, instead of the overwhelming situations which life presents.

Developing yourself is not a cakewalk, and you may need much patience to hang on. Ruining yourself, on the other hand, is very easy.

First we have to look deep into ourselves to see how we can destroy ourselves.

1. Negative attitudes.

   Thoughts are vital; what you think, you become. Whenever destructive thoughts try to sink in your mind, as a commander of yourself, you have to block them.Otherwise they will take control of your life and you will turn into a loyal soldier of those thoughts.

   Many talented people underperform because of their negative attitudes. They do not expect good things in life, due to their past setbacks, or other circumstances which they see and believe in. They think life is disorderly, utterly topsy-turvy, and that what they touch will go wrong. They never expect good things to happen.

2. Procrastination.

   It is easy to find something to kill valuable time which you will never be able to catch up with. Today's high tech innovations give you the boosters that enable you to procrastinate easily. Not working on your most important task, and working instead on less or not important tasks, is procrastination.

3. Negative relations.

   When you get on with negative relations, temporarily you may enjoy them. But when you look back, you will realize the emptiness of what you did, and how obstructive these have been. If you don't avoid naysayers in your life, they will distract you from major breakthroughs.

4. Settling with self.

   The moment you feel that what you have become is enough, you will stop growing, transcending, advancing or enjoying the adventure. When many of you achieve some things at a certain level, you feel there is nothing to do more. Relax your limitations for they block you from contributing something remarkable to solve the world's problems.

   Once you clearly identify these silent killers within you, go to the next step, and shoot them.

How do you do that?

1. Develop your mindset. Think positively, expect good things, and be optimistic. Try to get advantages from the problem which is torturing you. Get some help from prayers, meditation, goal reading and affirmations; they can be your seed capital to develop your mind business.
2. Develop physical value, health and fitness. Feeling good and energetic will lead you to completeness. Have pride in every part of your body. Take proper care. Enjoy proteins, vitamins and minerals necessary to supplement your food everyday, eat good things that make you happy and confident, and send signals to your mind that you are having good things, to avoid chances to get unwell. The message you transmit every time you exercise, and have good food and supplements, create subconscious convictions which keep you radiant and healthy.
3. Discover your hidden talents; you have more than one gift. When you look for yourself in your own invisible mental store, you will find many unused, valuable talents. Take them out and sharpen them by use. If you don't try to build a house of your success, using bricks of your talents, time will run out, keeping you in misery. In this life you have to use your talents to reveal your life's report in heaven.
4. Learn new skills, get some training, update your knowledge and intelligently direct them. In the span of our short lives, many things change fast, due to people who have control over industries and economy. If you don't keep up with new systems, update your knowledge and intelligently direct them for definite plans, you will find yourself in a dilemma.

In short, program your life's structure and use your days in full.

Memory count

1. Measure yourself honestly. Are you on the loser's side or the winner's side? Where do you really want to be? If you want to win, there should be no delay.
2. To understand the nature of all affairs of life, build a business, grow in your career, and have a fulfilling relationship are not easy because,

before you reach their standards, you will be rigorously tested. Pass the exam.

3. Monitor yourself. Are you getting ahead, day by day? There is no need to fly at the start; you can crawl. There is no need to know how to. Children crawl and finally stand and walk. Accept when you fall, but don't give up. Keep going.
4. There are people who own many materials, but lack the courage to multiply them. Show your confidence in starting things even with nothing. Your creative ideas will grow wings. Of course, the truth is that it's very hard.
5. The world is not always filled with difficult customers.People who have upgraded their human qualities towards a Godly nature will come to your side if you seek their help.
6. What holds you back? Find it and address it. Maybe it's your internal quality. Most of the time, you are your own enemy. Nobody can restructure your inner balance, except you.
7. Live life today onwards, day by day. Gather your energies, mental and physical, and fight with all the measures that you possess.
8. Act as if it were already done. Act strongly to prove that you deserve what you believe needs to be achieved.
9. Like attracts like; get miracles from the law of attraction. Always see and expect wonderful things, and you will receive them.

13

Make a mark

Just build your brand from day one, man. Your brand is your name, basically. A lot of people don't know that they need to build their brand; your brand is what keeps you moving.

Meek Mill

You can envisage how important one leader's vision to make a great mark was! Not only on our planet, but also on the moon! John F Kennedy proclaimed his vision and it was engraved in the hearts of the people in an unforgettable manner.

"But if I were to say, my fellow citizens, that we shall send to the moon, 240,000 miles away from the control station in Houston, a giant rocket more than 300 feet tall, the length of this football field, made of new metal alloys, some of which have not yet been invented, capable of standing heat and stresses several times more than have ever been experienced, fitted together with a precision better than the finest watch, carrying all the equipment needed for propulsion, guidance, control, communications, food and survival, on an untried mission, to an unknown celestial body, and then return it safely to earth, re-entering the atmosphere at speeds of over 25,000 miles per hour, causing heat about half that of the temperature of the sun — almost as hot as it is here today — and do all this, and do it right, and do it first before this decade is out — then we must be bold.

I'm the one who is doing all the work, so we just want you to stay cool for a minute. [Laughter]

However, I think we're going to do it, and I think that we must pay what needs to be paid. I don't think we ought to waste any money, but I think we ought to do the job. And this will be done in the decade of the sixties. It may be done while some of you are still here at school at this college and University. It will be done during the term of office of some of the people who sit here on this platform. But it will be done. And it will be done before the end of this decade."

What kind of conviction he had and what kind of conviction had been given to the nation! His clear, detailed explanation solidly sowed the seeds of the unshackling hopes of the followers, who determined to accomplish Kennedy's great vision, and succeeded in etching a significant mark in history, and writing a new chapter in the star wars.

Regardless of where you are working, in an organization, company, church ministry, political movement or a social meet up, image building and branding is vital. This is one of the common and decisive factors in the corporate world and marketing sector today.

What you want to become in the market of a particular organization is branding. Through your positioning you will metamorphose from a nobody to a somebody.

Your dress code, manners, communication, organizing skills, habits and behavior reflect what you represent. People don't buy your idea or product; they first buy you! And then your brand!

I have my own success stories to make you understand this simple concept.

Student movement

Where are you running? What is in your files?

Too busy, talking with each and every fresher! Very nice shirt!

These were the questions raised and statements made by some senior brothers and sisters in our faculty.

When I formed a new student movement in the Law Faculty in my University, with my fellow student members, many challenges loomed before us. How would we sell our ideology, while contesting with the long established students' movement, which was in power? There were a few minor issues against some student leaders, but they didn't seem crucial enough to evoke a change of power.

I branded myself.

I dressed up nicely even though I wasn't well off. It was a major highlight between the leaders of the student movements. Many wanted to represent the common people and they reflected that life style in their dressing too.They dressed simply and wore only slippers to show that they represented the common man. I walked fast, showing that I was spirited and enthusiastic. I was passionate about what I was doing.

A bunch of files was always with me, organized with all the documents related to student movements in Sri Lanka. I smiled at everyone and tried to make friends.

By my third year in the campus, I had never attended even one lecture. Hardly anyone knew me, except for a few people in my batch. I was working part time as a presenter in a TV station that belonged to the brother of the leader of a major political party in Sri Lanka.

When activists of the opposition party saw me all of a sudden, they branded me as a parachute man and the envoy of an outside party, who was trying to bring the ideology of the said party into the University. In order to justify their argument, they took my part time job and linked it with the political party. They were smart enough to plant bad impressions about me and many looked at me in a doubtful manner. I became a very controversial character, though popular. Our political movement grew beyond our expectations. Looking back, I now understand it was because of the branding strategy that I used unconsciously.

Next year we won the election and I became vice president of the student council in the University of Colombo.

Political career

It was rare that young politicians wore complete national dress in Sri Lanka. When I was to enter politics, the first thing I did was to make a national dress for myself. The reason was that my father used to wear the national dress when he went to attend special events in those days, and the image sank into my mind deeply. He looked very smart in that dress, and even though I was not a fair guy like him, it fit me well. I went to my district, wearing that dress to meet people in my first public gathering. I saw people came closer to me and they looked comfortable enough to get on with me. I attracted them very soon. Among all the candidates, they noticed something different in me. I was punctual, walked fast and quickly attended to them, wearing an infectious smile all the time, I showed them that I was different, and stood out from the others, and, hence, deserved a huge victory. Many people gave me a thumbs up and a huge support came from the young crowd. Especially from the ladies! It was my branding which I positioned there as a candidate. I became number one in that election.

Networking business

A neat and clean suit with branded ties and shoes made an impression on every one whom I prospected and associated with. Many wondered how

I kept my shoes clean in this condition amidst all the dust. I polished my shoes every morning until I could see my face in them. Wherever I went, I smiled at people as they spoke with me and initiated a dialogue. Even if I didn't get them involved in my business, I created a good relationship with them. I attended business meetings where many successful foreigners participated in the network marketing business. They assumed that I was already successful in this business. In fact, it was only the beginning and an intense learning period for me. I used all the products and showed myself as their brand ambassador, and people believed in the products. Due to some technical issues, foreign business owners were suspended temporarily. But I branded myself. In the process of achieving success through that business, I believe that I became someone worthwhile.

I noticed why many people underperform in their particular fields. They have no idea about how to sell themselves. If you work in a direct selling company which follows product leadership as a marketing strategy, you have to first be a consumer of your products, and not just use one or two products. You have to consume and experience all the products which you sell. When you are satisfied with your products, it is easy to share the benefits with another prospect. They will believe you, on seeing your face and body. For example, if you use protein and vitamin supplements, they will work on you and people who meet you often will understand the difference. Moreover, you will be confident enough to sell them.

Many people fail in this industry when they try to sell without trying the products. They strive to save money and maximize the profit, facing continuous loses. They turn into the enemies of the company which extended support to them to build their own business, mainly because they don't understand the fundamentals. If someone comes to you with a big stomach and tries to introduce a supplement which helps you to lose weight, what question will you raise first? You will ask, "Why don't you use these products?" You can't give excuses saying that you can't control your sugar intake. If you say so, you may lose the business.

I once met one guy who was good at sales and gifted with talents. But he couldn't ever reach his expectations. Not able to fathom the reason, he always complained that people in the market did not understand the value of the products. I realized why he was not reaching his level; it was because he never reached people on time. He didn't understand the value of time, and so he was not punctual. He lacked a major characteristic which could enhance the quality of his talent. He had very bad brand identity; he was always late.

I noticed a very industrious guy who prospected people every day. He would show his business plan to everyone he met with demos of the products. He got customers but lost out as they did not buy from him a second time, because he tried to make small profits without giving back the balance money of the products which he sold. Some people came to look for him several times as he had borrowed some money from them and not returned it. He lost his brand image as he didn't possess integrity.

Another time I met a guy who was working for an MNC and wanted to build his own business through multi level marketing. He had a sound knowledge of marketing, and his communication skills were excellent. But he did not want to go that extra mile. He joined the business and came up with unrealistic proposals which were against the ethics and damaged the structure of the business. He proved to be a lazy brand.

Put your heart, mind, and soul into even your smallest acts. This is the secret of success.

Swami Sivananda

Your brand is your public identity, what you're trusted for. And for your brand to endure, it has to be tested, redefined, managed, and expanded as markets evolve. Brands either learn or disappear.

Lisa Gansky

I think what I do in my acting world and what I do in my standup world is bring up a brand that I want to bring across. Once you figure out your brand and what you do, it's kind of easy at that. You end up getting your audience.

J. B. Smoove

You can make a mark and brand yourself before leaving this planet by living life in full but a bit for yourself, and much for others.

Keerthisinghe

Memory count

1. Do your best to communicate with the hearts of people. Before you shake their hands, permanently accommodate yourself in their hearts. This is valid in your personal, professional and spiritual life.
2. Prepare well, but take care not to overdo the preparation. Your preparation will reflect from your face, from your eye contact and

body postures. Words will flow tirelessly and effortlessly. I noticed in my presentations and business meetings that, when I was well prepared, I did well. However, when my preparation was poor, my performance and outcome went down. Thorough preparation creates a good impression. There is no need to be perfect, but try to make the preparation a complete experience.

3. Your qualities will bring forth expected quantities, and will attract a number of people and resources. Show integrity and be honest.
4. Claim victory always and it will follow you. Never surrender to 'No'. Don't associate with negative vibes.
5. Show leadership qualities, and always love, protect, direct, provide and sacrifice, regardless of where you are working and what you are doing.
6. Be influential and show teachability. Organize knowledge every day, coming a life time learner. Establish a mark of humility
7. Work on your strength zones, day and night, for maximum deliverance. It will bring great results to you and help you make a mark. Show your expertise.
8. Show that you are ready to reproduce. Clone your character.
9. Cultivate generosity and never be a person who eats alone.
10. Dress in your best clothes, according to the occasion. People will admire you and seek your company.
11. Give a message to others that they can trust you and depend on you, and on your product or service.
12. Always try to see things through your mind's eye and be sensible. Show things to others so that they can observe with their naked eyes. Be a creator and initiator.

My pay check is important for my living, my self esteem is important to make me alive.

Keerthisinghe

14

My mind saw many things before my eyes

Whatever we plant in our subconscious mind, and nourish with repetition and emotion, will one day become a reality.

Earl Nightingale

A Relationship that enlightened my life

It was one day in April 1997, when I ran into a person with a charming smile, in front of the Faculty of Law Library. She glanced at me and revealed her musical voice slowly.

"How are you? I haven't seen you in a long time!" I couldn't recall her, but my heart nudged me, "You know her."

I just smiled and replied, "I'm fine. Was busy with some work, which is why I haven't been here in a long time"

While talking, I observed her features carefully.

Long hair, talking eyes, tan color, perfectly created teeth, wide hips with a dancing walk. Who was she? I asked my heart, and again, my heart said, "You know her." She attracted me from the first moment.

I forgot the purpose for which I had gone to my University that day.

"If you have time, we can talk over a drink," she said.

There was a nice cafe adjoining our faculty. Hours flew without notice as we talked about many things.

She revealed very honestly that she had a crush on me.

She had never missed any TV program which I had presented. She had fallen in love with me even without knowing me.

When I had addressed my fellow students, while leading the students' movement, she had heard all my speeches, and silently supported us. While giving my speech, I had endured a tough challenge from the opposition party, as they had jumped onto the stage and tried to take my microphone away by force. I clung on to the microphone, so they that they couldn't pull it away from my hand. I had no idea how I got that miraculous power as many people tried to prevent me from speaking. I continued amidst their noisy disruptions, speaking till the very end. I became a hero in one moment, and many praised my courage. I had always challenged my opposition counterpart to have a debate with me, but he had kept avoiding it. I lost that election, but I realized that I had won her heart. She said it was that very moment her heart painted my photo colorfully. I understood the value of real love in life. It was not an illusion or a breakable thing, but a romantic story which could be written in books.

I never thought of leaving her. Yes, even today I have not left her. She will come to me again in my very first book and she will live there forever. But in reality, in an unexpected moment, we were separated by fate. Even though I was not fond of that word 'fate', I couldn't find any word in the English dictionary apt enough to illustrate that unfortunate incident. Till the end of time, until my heartbeat stops, that memory won't die in my heart.

Again, I sink back into that memory. My heart said, "You know her!" when I saw her for the first time, closely and face to face. How? I recalled my memories of my teenage life. I had grown up in a big family. On the same land, we had two houses; one was old and the other was new, built by my father at that time. My father had five brothers and six sisters. We lived together in those houses.

Many of my father's sisters inherited natural beauty. His eldest sister was not only incredibly pretty, but also very kind and caring to everyone. She had all the qualities, externally and internally, to become a good life partner, but unfortunately she had no faith in men and hence, was not interested in getting married.

The process started spontaneously. When I saw her, I thought that I needed a person with similar features and a good heart like her. It was not a simple thought but one that was deeply rooted in my mind with a detailed description. Even the way she talked and walked, her long hair, her charming personality, complexion and everything about her! The mental photograph of my future life partner resembled her. My objective mind collected all those details carefully and sent them to my subjective mind. My subjective mind, day and night, sought her and finally made her stand in front of me. After reading great literature written on the wonderful power of the subconscious mind, I understood the magic working power of the mind. What authors explained in their books was really true and scientific.

Behind all our major achievements or failures, our thoughts play a very important role, one which is impressed in our subconscious mind. My honest life experiences are witness to this true principle. When they become subconscious convictions, results come to the surface.

Election

The jailor came with a small piece of paper and put it on my palm. I unfolded it. 24864. I had won the first election which I contested in the Provincial Legislature to become number one. I couldn't be in the counting centre because of a shooting incident. We were remanded on the last day of the election. I was in remand prison for 23 days and my supporters were there for 90 days.

After 13 years, I had come back to my district to contest for the said election. Only a few recalled me. How did I get such huge support and finance for that election? How did I make it a creative campaign? Not only did I design lucrative posters and tapes, but I also ran a well organized and creative campaign. Even before I started the campaign, I became number one in my mind, prior to the nomination. How did I get the nomination when many believed that I wouldn't? Even the three parliamentarians and all the organizers of the district had opposed it. It was 2 am in the morning. I was in the party head quarters seeking a nomination. The list was about to be finalized. There was no place for me.

Finally, the party leader and the nomination committee noticed that one member was missing. They inquired from an ex-minister about what had happened to his candidate. He told them that he was on the way. Then the leader said, "Let's enlist Keerthi as a standby." Later after the election, the party leader met me in a leadership work shop held to train us for TV shows, and he said, "Keep smiling! The standby man has become number one! Great job! Now I have to make the district leaders befriend you."

Before my name came to the list, I knew I was there. It was my subconscious conviction. Even though I didn't have an understanding about those principles, I imagined the declaration of my nomination.

Before the election commissioner declared my victory, I declared to myself and to my close well wishers about my victory, and that I surely I would become number one. It was my mental deposit which became a reality. Day and night, until I achieved that victory, memorizing and visualizing the accomplishment, I ran the campaign.

Many people were amazed, and many others assumed that my victory happened because of money power. I didn't have party support at all, and the three parliamentarians, who represented my district, fought with me and ran parallel campaigns to defeat me.

When I recalled this eleven year old memory, my heart confirmed that all the things which had occurred to me were due to my strong subconscious convictions.

Cut Off Marks

261. This was the cut off mark to enter the faculty of law in the 1991 advance level examination for the university entrance from my district. I had exactly what it required, not a single mark more. Had I got one mark less, I would have not been a lawyer. Everybody said I was lucky. Today I believe it was not my luck. I was the only student who got selected from my school to enter the university. There were many brighter students than me. In Economics, I got an A pass. For two subjects, Political Science and Buddhist Civilization, I had no tutors.

I had a great dream to become a lawyer, even before I entered that advanced level class. That desire was strongly imprinted in my subconscious mind. I decorated my faith, visualizing and wearing the dress of a lawyer in my mind. That belief and mental work paid off. With minimal facilities, without doing very hard work, and even after engaging in extra activities in the school, I achieved that which I wanted badly.

It was really a miracle. My relatives knew me as a stubborn person, who didn't normally listen to the opinions of the adults. Complaints had flowed from different people. But my mind power was more powerful than others' opinions of me. My conscious mind was not ready to get defeated at that time. That positive mindset must have sunk into my subconscious mind. When I didn't have teachers for two subjects, my mind directed me to follow two guide books which I bought from the City Book Shop. While walking to school with very little pocket money from my grandmother, I was attracted to the picture of the University of Colombo, the only university that had a Faculty of Law at that timc in Sri Lanka.

Life Style

Habits become subconscious convictions, which are good or bad, positive or negative. Because the subconscious doesn't have the rational power to argue with your conscious thoughts, it can only obey your conscious commands and thoughts. When I began to earn on my own, I thought that I should only wear the best brands in the market. Wherever I went, I bought whatever I wanted for myself. Even when I gift something to someone, I still do the same. If I give something to a beggar even, I give him sufficient money to fulfill his hunger for one meal. Even when I was in financial doldrums, I used to do window shopping. I would try on things, and if I really liked them, I would build my desire on them spontaneously. When I wore them, a feeling of joy would peep into my mind! I found that if I really needed certain things, there were many occasions in my life, when I received those things as gifts at unexpected moments. There were times I didn't have money to buy something at a particular moment; but, without delay, money would come to enable me to buy the desired thing. It became my mental habit, in fact, and not my exaggeration.

When I want to eat something or chill, I never settle for anything average. Even though I can adjust with situations, I prefer to have healthy, better quality things. This doesn't mean that I want to throw around money unnecessarily. It is richness which I have deposited in my subconscious, and always it is on the job to find me avenues to accomplish things in that nature. I always like to be in a joyful state of mind. It comes to me even in these little material forms. Every day, from the time I get up until I go to sleep, and even in my dreams, I strive for happiness, joy, peace, wealth and power. I strongly believe and cultivate in my subconscious, and sooner or later, I get avalanches of abundance.

Now to him that is able to do exceeding abundantly, above all that we ask or think, according to the power that works in us.

Ephesians 3: 20 American King James Version

My heart exults with this verse in the Bible in sheer joy. I don't worry because if I have sufficient conviction coupled with belief, it turns into the power that works in us. What else? I always believe that I will get everything I want and that, day by day, I will prosper beyond the limits. That power that works in us is super natural and I got the connection by harnessing belief in my heart.

According to the Buddha and scientific researches, there are many thoughts that flow into our minds every day. If we carefully select them for our betterment and the betterment of the society as a habit, they will convince our subconscious mind. In Pali and Sanskrit, I believe the Buddha named this as 'sammā-sati' - Right Mindfulness. If you possess and develop this, you will always attract good things. The Buddha preaches that you can achieve this through 'sammā kammanta'- through right action or right conduct that lead to good business, profession or career. According to Jesus, this comes through faith, and according to scientific research, it is due to subconscious conviction through strongly cultivated belief.

Travel to Kanagawa City

In 2007, I visited Japan. It was my fifth visit to Japan and my first visit to Kanagawa City. I stayed in a hotel there. I had never visited the city earlier, but when I was walking around, I felt that I had seen the building and features of the city somewhere before. It gave me a very close and familiar memory, a sense of déjà vu! Suddenly I recalled that before I came there, I had a dream in which I saw all the things which I was now seeing in reality. How did it happen? I had not even seen a photo of Kanagawa City before. Yet, I can understand how it happened. Some dreams give us inklings as a result of subconscious activity. Today I believe this through my own experience.

Closing down my travel company

At the end of the completion of the fifth year, I was compelled to close down my travel company due to its unsuccessful performance. When I got into politics, I used to think that that was not my line of business. I needed to focus full time on politics. I also strongly believed that no one in my family could focus on this, apart from me. I always thought that my employees would not give me good support. I felt that they would initiate some harmful practices in the company. They really did so. This mirrored my conscious mind's belief which the subconscious mind brought forth into reality. Thus, we have to be very careful about our thoughts. They can cause disastrous damage in our life.

Temporary Break from Politics

"Again, truly I tell you that if two of you on earth agree about anything they ask for, it will be done for them by my Father in heaven."

Matthew 18:19

Here, an agreement between the two of you refers to your conscious belief and subconscious acceptance. When both are in agreement, results will pour out from our heavenly father.

One day I met a horoscope reader through my friend. He was a lecturer in a University. He predicted that, given the period that I was going through, there was a huge possibility that something could happen to my life while I was in a big crowd. Being a politician, I attended many rallies in those days. From time to time, his prediction came to my mind, at night before I slept. And when I got up in the morning, it left me with an incredibly bad impact. Without my knowledge, my mind found many excuses to get away from my daily routine. I even doubted that my party leader would replace me in my constituency. Some gossip mongers who brought me negative and false information attracted me. I started to argue with certain leaders of the party. In the bargain, I started to dislike my political career. I criticized my party leader publicly on television, supporting the then ruling party. My party removed me from all responsibilities. My subconscious had smartly found a way to put me aside.

After two years, my colleagues represented the same assembly which I had represented, and most of the big political figures in my area died in a bomb blast. If I had been there, this book wouldn't be in your hand today.

I don't intend to promote a belief in horoscopes in this paragraph; horoscopes become 'horrorscopes' many times. But my subconscious was clever enough to save me for the future by avoiding the great tragedy that could have taken away my life.

'I will instruct you and teach you in the way you should go I will guide with my eye. Do not be like the horse or mule which has no understanding.'

Psalm32:8, 9

Psalms beautifully define the Divine power and how it connects with us. God's eye is invisible, creative and can see the whole Universe. The power the creator has planted in our subconscious mind has a great understanding which other animals don't possess. 'I will guide you with my eye' means that you will get support from your creative intelligence within you, that unique feature which has been created by God only in humans.

Our subconscious minds have no sense of humor, play no jokes and cannot tell the difference between reality and an imagined thought or image. What we continually think about eventually will manifest in our lives.

Robert Collier

Only one thing registers on the subconscious mind: repetitive application - practice. What you practice is what you manifest.

Fay Weldon

You will be a failure, until you impress the subconscious with the conviction you are a success. This is done by making an affirmation which 'clicks.'

Florence Scovel Shin

Memory count

1. What are the thoughts that come to the surface of your mind? Monitor them every day and check if they are in your favor. If they make you rich and happy, or bring you enthusiasm, consciously nurture them through repetition.
2. Focus on the one event that you desire strongly in reality in the future and take a mental picture, in the same manner as a professional photographer focuses the frame to capture your image, very carefully, with much effort. Sometimes the photographer shoots different angles to choose the best of you. Likewise, choose the best for yourself and send the picture to your subconscious mind for the process.
3. Constantly think of what you have deposited in your deep mind and practice it. Send happy signals on your progress to your subconscious mind, to propel you forward through perseverance for an ultimate accomplishment in greater size.
4. Belief is the law of life. When you believe with sufficient conviction, it will bring forth the expected results; you can never convince your mind with fear and doubt. The Bible says to present your case. You have to present your case to the Lord and believe; in other words, you can submit your case in the mode of images to your subconscious mind, accept and feel strongly that they are true, to see the miracles.
5. Once you understand the inner power and invisible wonders within you, you have to be careful about your habits, thoughts, words and actions. If they form good habits, systems and routings, you can water and make them fertile or else terminate them. When your habitual actions make subconscious convictions according to nature, results will follow.
6. When you write down your goals on paper and repeat them several times a day, pictures and vivid messages will sink into your subconscious mind, and find ways to solve the contradiction with reality and imagery. Because of this strong conviction, all the required resources will amazingly align with your dream to transmute it into reality, sooner or later.

7. You can declare your victory to yourself before it happens and organize your happy feeling about it. Through the law of attraction, victory will be yours.
8. Through specific and simple prayer, you can bring forth results. Observe the answered state of your request through imagination, and enable it to be an impression in your subconscious mind. Affirm your prayer, without the mental congestion of fear and doubt, according to your faith.
9. You are the architect of your mind palace, and you can choose to decide everything. You can change, replace and consciously build exactly what you want, with the help of the giant power within your subconscious mind.
10. Your subconscious is at its active best at the time before you sleep and after you awake. Think clearly and make use of the opportunity to receive extraordinary things in life.
11. Visualization is the best mental exercise; so practice it frequently. This will activate your creative faculty, and through the reticular activating system in your brain, you can find unused resources, and also magnetize the required sources to achieve your desired dreams and goals.
12. Based on uncertain fear, never impregnate pictures of making the ends meet, close downs and bankruptcy in your brain cells. Instead, throughout your life, sow and reap prosperity.

15

Spirit Flows, Power Glows

It was quite late at night, when I came home after finishing my long day. Nothing had worked out according to my expectations. So many disappointments and rejections in one day! My emotional health had gone down drastically. My mind was frozen and my head was numb. I kept my bag on the table in front of my bed, the bag which I used to carry every day when I went out for meetings. I just lay down on the bed without removing my shoes and said to myself, "Oh my God, life is not easy!" I looked at my bag made of good leather, which had been with me for ages. It looked worn out and overloaded. I felt that it was staring at me in anger. I responded that that I also didn't like it. "I am fed up with you!" I didn't take my eyes from it for some time. I imagined my bag and I were really the same. Overloaded!

I carry a heavy baggage within me since the day I understood a bit about life. It's always overloaded, and the journey is tiresome. My bag doesn't have a proper place to be in; when I go by metro, I put it down; when I hold meetings, it is sometimes on the table or on the ground next to my chair. Sometimes I give it to someone to hold. It is filled with all kinds of things - papers, pens, books, card holders, mouth freshener, thermos, tablets, tapes and much more. My life is also like that. Like good leather; stretchable and expanding. My life has no proper place to stand, but is just moving. Sometimes just hanging somewhere! I let some people hold some areas in my life. Sometimes my thought patterns hold me.

My life also is filled with impediments, setbacks, worries, failures, hardships, toxic relations, unlimited responsibilities and unfinished tasks, and somewhere in the corner, big dreams which I don't have the courage and energy to fuel. When I rested this bag by replacing it with a new bag, my heart questioned me, "Hey, man, what's next? When are you going to add something to your life after putting down your heavy sack?" I answered angrily, "What else remains to be done? I can't put my baggage away!" My heart laughed, "Why don't you? Clean it. Put unnecessary things into the trash, and keep only the essentials for the journey. If you carry less weight, it is easy to climb, even if it is another mountain." Wise advice, indeed!

I got up from the bed, rushed to the bag and took everything out. I threw out old torn papers and books, pens which couldn't be used, put in only one note pad, one pen, only very important books and checked the weight again. Much less and much better! I felt the bag was smiling at me. No longer would I need to put it down everywhere.

I went to the mirror and talked to myself. "Release your luggage, release your talents, choose some skills and train them until you become master of the same." Then I went to the shower and enjoyed it for more than forty minutes until I had washed out all the negativity. Some faces appeared before me when I closed my eyes in the shower. Many people whom I had met today had said, "Fine!" Were they truly fine? Their eyes said otherwise. Obviously they didn't mean it. Some of them were unable to keep eye contact when they said fine. Some had very pale hopeless faces, and looked fed up; others scratched their heads, looked at me, trying to evince fake smiles. I said to myself, "Not just you, but many people are not fine yet." While having my shower, I committed to myself that I would unload the anger which I held against my enemies, and undo the regrets and worries which held me back. I repeated to myself that I should monitor my words.

What are the words you use throughout the day? Are they positive or negative? Whatever they are, the important thing is that when you read or speak these words loudly, the emotions attached to them will slowly move to your heart, and change your mood in a blink of an eye. That is the power of those words that you use frequently. They affect you and the moods of others around you.

What are your favorite activities which make your day and bring you alive while you engage in them? How many of you listen to your inner voice? If you do so, you will find your purpose of life. Why should we have our own personal conversations? The reason is we all have inner questions to clarify, most of which cannot be answered by anyone else. Primarily because you are the one who knows and understands your own self more than others do.

We all have our own unique features, physical and mental. Even your loved ones may not be able to decipher your feelings on many occasions. If you want to see unprecedented miracles in life, let your inner thoughts come out. One effective way to do this is to use your free time to allow your mind to empty all its thoughts and let it get instilled with fresh ones.

In order to get relaxation, most of us use wrong methods. It is imperative not to complicate your leisure time with your mind relaxation time, which is when you have to deliberately do some restructuring to your mental house, with necessary refurbishments.

In your leisure time, you can share your happy thoughts with someone else. As far as mind relaxation goes, it is important to share your thoughts with your inner person, with whom you should have an intelligent mind session. You should have this mind vacation every day for at least a few minutes, as it is inexpensive and result oriented. It is almost as though you will be able to get reincarnation without physical body departure. Enormous opportunities will appear, beyond the limits of your capabilities. This mental exercise will help you grow, start your life with full speed and bring fruitful experiences to you and people around you. Sudden change can happen in your life even if you have tried hard earlier and not succeeded. While most of us are eager to find solutions from experts and friends to change our lives, it is necessary to have self conversation for fast and immediate change. Nobody can change your weight, health, career, finances and relations. Only you can do it.

I decided to do a simple child like exercise after my shower. I got a pen and paper and wrote down a list.

My complaints:

1. Our educational system
2. Politicians and Governments
3. Economy
4. People
5. My loved ones
6. Myself

I trashed the paper.

I thought about successful people in the world and the hardships that they had undergone. Many were homeless, some slept on the streets before they built their financial empires, some didn't have proper college education, and some were abandoned by their biological parents. Most were nobodies, nowhere! I was in a better place when compared to them. If they could do something significant in their lives, why couldn't I? Why couldn't I be what I wanted to be? How did they achieve such elevated levels? How did they spend their time productively? What did they carry within them always? I realized I was still not too late. I felt motivated more than ever before. Having cleaned my mental room as well as I could, I went to sleep, releasing the pillow which I used to hold tightly before. For a change, I slept peacefully, holding my dreams tightly. I felt that my dreams were embracing me more lovingly than ever before.

Next day, I woke up a little early. I felt a big burst of energy in me. My mind was light, almost refilled with new and hopeful thoughts. I thanked God for everything that He had planted in me, as also my parents for their genes. Because of them, I genetically possessed some talents and qualities. I also gave thanks to some people who had helped me in my adverse times. And as usual, my enemies came to mind. I said loudly, "Live long to see my massive success one day!"

Then I jumped out of bed and stood in front of the mirror. Feeling good, I said to myself, "This is my day; think, man, of what you have in you! Release your talents freely. You have the right to be rich, happy and successful. You can do it. No matter how tough it is, until you see what you want before your eyes, you will have to make strenuous efforts." Thus, I made a firm commitment to myself.

Then I sat and wrote down my goals in detail with expected dates for them to be achieved. If I had showed them to someone, they would definitely have told me that my goals were not possible to achieve. I hadn't written anything that normal persons couldn't achieve in their lifetime. Many people had done so through their efforts. There are people who judge people according to their own past failures and current monetary situations. I had also downgraded the efforts of others sarcastically when I was immature earlier.

Whenever a new idea or plan struck me, I immediately acted and shared it with my friends or prospects. Sometimes I presented many plans to the same people from time to time. The good thing was that they were keen to listen to me, even though they didn't show any initiative to go ahead with it. Most of the time, I met people at the coffee house or over lunch or dinner. I used to invite them to have something with me and share what I intended to start. When they saw my enthusiasm in presenting the idea, they hesitated to ask me about the ideas I had come up with equal enthusiasm earlier.

Many asked me at the end of our one on one meets, "How do you keep up your enthusiasm and remain so spirited?"

I would answer clearly and firmly, "Fail several times in your life, but still, if you can stand with faith, you will feel that you have big dreams to achieve. Spirit gets generated from the high level of confidence you entertain. In my life, there are many more things to be accomplished. I can't let anything shake my confidence."

Memory count

1. Be alert about your mental hygiene. Your emotional health and vitality are very important. Clean your mental house, and make necessary repairs. You have to care about your physical health every day. The same care and treatment should be given to your mind as well. Don't watch horror movies and news items which contain criminal scenes before you sleep, as they will sink down to your deep mind, leaving you with depleted energy when you wake up.
2. One by one, release those unbearable deposits which cause mental congestion and lead to physical disorders. Anger, doubts, fear, regrets and disappointments are on the wrong side of life. Don't retain them in your mind's stock.
3. Empty your whole mental house for a while, take time off to relax and get the sincere support of your heart, along with support from the Almighty above.
4. Reload positive and nourishing thoughts; meditation will help you in this process. Your mind will enjoy good thoughts, which are good mind supplements.
5. Once you get up in the morning, align with spiritual energies, be thankful to your creator and give gratitude to everyone who has extended their supportive hands to you. Once your mind is filled with your spiritual energy, your body begins to reflect the positive signs that make your whole day come alive. You will remain happy and enthusiastic.
6. In your prayers, expect wonderful things throughout the day, believe in continued protection, and supply for yourself and your loved ones. Be specific with your prayers and avoid conflicting mental pictures and feelings. Try to see the answered state of your prayers in your mind.
7. Value the creative ideas which come through hunches. Don't forget to write them down and keep them safe. Some ideas are extremely useful and indispensable. They will help you to make a fortune and live life with abundance.

8. Meet the most valuable person in the morning before you meet anyone - yourself! See yourself in the mirror and make a lovely affirmation. Avoid talking with someone who makes your blood boil even on the phone in the morning.

   "I love myself and like the way I am. Wonderful things are happening today in my favor. I am spiritful, and creative forces are raining over me. I am blessed and all is well."

9. Read your written goals to imprint them in your mind, giving some reminders about deadlines. Don't turn on Facebook or multimedia social sites until evening, and don't spend time with unnecessary emails and news items. Read something related to your field which adds to your specialty and progress. Listen to motivational messages.

10. Have lunch with someone who can offer you some values; maybe your spouse, a friend, a coach or a teacher. Avoid the naysayers who pull your leg and say, "You can't."

11. Make practical and effective use of the day, personally, professionally and spiritually. Try to do something different and creative.

12. Help someone at least with your words, don't turn away from needy people, but contribute some time voluntarily. It will heighten your self esteem.

13. The Buddha preached this valuable generosity in The First Paramita: 'Dana' in Pali which means Generosity.

14. Service of all kinds, helping others, often giving ourselves through our heart:

Risk everything, even your name and reputation. Don't risk your generosity, as it will bring back your name and reputation one day.

Keerthisinghe

16

The way you see things

Attitude is a little thing that makes a big difference.

Winston Churchill

Attitude makes a difference between losers and winners, people who want to survive and who want to thrive. It makes a difference between managers and leaders, attenders and pretenders.

One evening, when I was in class two, I was doing some handicraft work assigned by my class teacher, using clay at home. My father came to me after his work, patted my head lovingly and asked, "My big son, what are you doing?"

I said, "I am trying to make an animal from this clay."

He said, "Stop this clay work."

I looked at him. He said in a very convincing way, "I want you to be an engineer, not a craftsman who makes things in clay. You know what I am doing?"

I said, "Yes, you are a government contractor."

"Right! Listen, son, you have to be an engineer of the Irrigation Department one day. I work with engineers and I know how valuable and prestigious that profession is. You better go to your aunty. She knows mathematics very well. Learn that subject and leave aside this clay work."

Next day, I went to school and the teacher asked for the homework from every student. He called out my name and asked me, "Did you do your home work?" I stood up quickly, and said, "No, sir, my father said doing clay work is not worthy. He asked me to be an engineer." The teacher knew my father well. He just smiled at me and all the students started to laugh.

He said, **"You can't be what you want to be, but you will be someone if you learn something."**

I didn't want to take his opinion. My father is my hero and he had told me something different. Again, in the evening, my father came with well ripened good quality bananas and handed me one, asking how things had gone in school. I told him about what the teacher had said,

"You can't be what you want to be, but you will be someone if you learn something."

He laughed. My father didn't have a high school education, but he was fluent in English. He read English newspapers every day and used to narrate the stories which were written in the children's section.

He asked, "Do you want to be an engineer?"

I said, "Yes."

"Then you can be. I will make you what I want you to be."

His voice gave me some sort of hidden command at that time. He continued, "You had better learn mathematics well from your aunt." I slowly got my books and went to see my aunt, his sister, who had a city school education and was good at mathematics. My father died after a few months in an accident. Later I understood my father hadn't underestimated that clay work. It was his attitude, and the way he saw things. He saw things as they were and he realized the potential in the country, being an engineer. Even today, only a few professions are recognized in Sri Lanka, which have economical and market value. Being a craftsman may have some sentimental value, but no other potential. I couldn't be an engineer by profession, according to his dream, but I became an engineer of my life, having designed and created my own model in life today. If he was with us today, he would be very happy.

Your life is your living enterprise, your heart is the reception and mind is the warehouse. Doing a warm welcome in your reception and storing only the good things in a neat and clean way in your mental warehouse, will bring you success.

Keerthisinghe

What do you think about the above statement? Your life is your business. It is your duty to work on it, day and night, making a 100% effort to maximize its effect and spread it everywhere to make it huge. What is vital is to see how you accept things and keep them in your store, until you get customers and make profit out of your life. Also, I stress here the importance of having an entrepreneurial mindset to achieve anything in life. In short, all achievements, regardless of their nature, generate profits. Profits can come as a monetary value or an intangible value, like name and fame, happiness and joy.

How do you perceive this world? What is your attitude towards it? Do you see it with your brain or feel it with your heart? If you feel it with your heart, you will love it, and be kind to this world. You will accept everything which this planet gifts to you, lovingly and wholeheartedly. Even some hard things you will tolerate with patience as you will be others centered, and because you believe that this wonderful creation is specifically designed by the master craftsman. Loving kindness, compassion and generosity are the materials used in this creation. When you embrace things in this manner, you will always think of creating something to gift back to this world as gratitude towards God. That is how you get the tendency to find and release your talents.

If you think from your brain and make and arguments about how it happened, you will not respect nature and values, but always think of creation of the world as a process, taking everything for granted. Then it will be like processed food, less in nutrition and high in health risks.

We need to think about human life as a wonderful creation of God.

"You shall love your neighbor as yourself." There is no other commandment greater than this.

Jesus Christ

The Buddha's teaching doesn't assume that the world is a creation of God. The Buddha is one of the mightiest prophets who understood and envisioned the changes in the generations of this world. He taught how to cultivate compassion in people who have knowledge in their brains. According to the Buddha, it's a science. Science is knowledge about things as they are.

Visualizing people you love and giving out this good feeling to them; then doing the same with people you love less, until you might even feel compassion for people you hate.

Maitri Bhawana – The Buddha

Whatever we do for a living in this world, ultimately, our heart yearns to find happiness and peace. In life, we experience many things other than success. Often failures, worries and regrets enter the reception of our living enterprise. We can't refuse them entry or send them back. But being the owners of the enterprise, we have every right to store in our warehouse only selected, good things.

Richness, confidence, happiness and hopes have good price tags, all in abundance. If you want them in a small size or in a great size, you will not pay the price. They are mental states. Entertain big hopes, not small ones. Try to do everything with passion and compassion. When you possess a blend of this energy booster and love booster automatically, you will drive wherever you want to, and become what you want to be. Love and compassion are decisive factors that govern this amazing human race.

It is our duty to see things in a positive way and attitude. That positive mind is the padlock of our mental warehouse. Once we see everything positively, we put the padlock, so that the negativity cannot enter. Even if they try a counter attack, you can do a mind recondition therapy to eradicate those invaders. Every morning through prayers, goal readings and affirmations, you can instill a positive pressure on your brain cells.

Everything we create and do is based on our thinking, based on how we see and receive things. If we could decorate our mind with the right mental attitude, no one or nothing can prevent the achievement of the goals in our dreams. Similarly, if someone refuses to remove the cloth of negativity from his mental body, nobody will be able to help him achieve those things. It's personal. You have the control as you are the engineer of your model.

If successful people open out their hearts and minds, you will perceive their attitude towards their life first. They see this life as an opportunity, and one that they have come here to win. That right attitude leads them to attract all positive things in life, and consequently, all departments of their lives will flourish. They become very charismatic leaders, magnifying everyone and everything that they are willing to own.

Our personal, social and professional departments of life are interconnected. Our attitude in one department will automatically flow to another. Some people see life as an accident, and others think that life is a punishment. They live because they can't die by themselves. They just get by, as they have the personal lives that they bring forth when they get married and raise a family. If they are influenced positively by their partners, they may change their attitude. Or else, they might plant their negative attitude onto the other. Their kids grow under the influence of the family surroundings. Very rarely do some move away from this condition. What happens when people, who hold a negative attitude, get involved with the society? They carry it forward with them in their work, and in their careers.

I met a rich industrialist one day. Actually, I prospected him for my new business. At that time I was working as a network marketer, and was associated with a multi level marketing company that dealt with some amazing products, including food supplements. I showed him the sales and marketing plans knowing that he was a rich guy. While he was sipping his coffee, he seemed impatient, judging by the expression on his face, but I pretended not to notice his displeasure. He interrupted me when I was presenting the plan and said, "I am not interested. I don't have anything to prove. I am well-off. I have four houses to be given to my four children and more than hundreds are working for me. Money is not important for me." He sounded arrogant and rejected me outright.

I said, "Sir, can I ask you one question?" He said, "Go ahead."

"What is your social contribution?" I asked.

"I am not a social guy. So I have nothing to do with that," he said.

I said, "Why, don't you think that you could contribute something to children who are needy? This company which I am associating with does many things for children."

He said there were enough people to do so and that he didn't want to do anything.

"What about animals?"

"What should I do for animals? I have two dogs at home and my servants feed them."

"You can, perhaps, do something for the environment, trees, the soil, water, the earth." I made this comment, continuing, "Being an industrialist, you are party to so many activities that pollute the earth."

He said he had no time to think about these silly things.

"Can I ask you one more question?"

He said, "You can ask hundreds, but I will not join you."

I said, "It's ok. Sir, have you done something special for your employees?"

He said, "What else? I pay them a salary."

"Sir, do you have a health plan? Are you regularly doing exercise and taking adequate rest? Are you using good food supplements?"

He said, "What for?"

I said, "Thank you very much for your time, sir." I rushed to the counter, paid the bill and moved away. I didn't say, "See you!" to him because I didn't want to see his attitude towards life.

There are simple examples galore to explain the nature of self centered characters. Go to the coffee house and observe how people occupy tables in a restaurant. Individuals occupy big tables. Even though they see people who come in a group, rarely do they offer the big table to them by moving to a smaller one. People wish to be comfortable, disregarding the inconvenience of others. Sometimes their omissions, at other times their actions, make others uncomfortable. What about people who smoke in public? Why don't they think about others, especially kids? It is due to their attitude. Some attitudes are harmful not only for them, but also for others, and for the sustainability of this earth.

When I stepped out of the mall, someone smiled at me. We shook hands and exchanged cards. "I will call him and make an appointment tomorrow," I said to myself, "I refuse to accept others' rejections on my proposals as my problem. It's their problem and their lack of vision. Not everybody can see what dream drivers see."

People who have a positive attitude, irrespective of financial backgrounds, cultivate their attitude in the soil of their family, society, work and career by donating tremendous fruits to the planet, as a return for the investments granted to them by nature.

My employee's attitude

A popular movie star was jailed and my employee was saddened. To add to that, she attempted to justify the injustice he had done. She gave me her reasons. "He has done his bit for the country and he shouldn't be jailed."

I asked her a question. "How do you distinguish the value of the lives that died because of his activity from the value of this movie star's life?" She was unhappy to hear the question. "Who knows whether the people who died would have delivered something to this country if they had been alive for the next ten twenty years?" I continued.

She said, "But…?"

I asked the second harsh question. "If the victims had belonged to your family, what would you have done? Would you have tolerated it?"

She kept silent, but her attitude was revealed on her face. She said again after some time, "He should appeal."

After a while, another topic arose. I said that people who were doing bad business also celebrated success, but they would not prevail in happiness for long. Then I continued, "I have a Buddhist back ground, and I feel that there are a few businesses which shouldn't be conducted, including that of liquor."

She said, "Liquor is needed by people."

I asked a torturous question again. "If your husband is drunk and beats you in front of your children, what would you feel?"

She said, "Without liquor also, people do so."

"That is right!" I replied. That's the attitude of a person who is looking for success. I reminded her of the importance of success with significance, namely contributing something good to society.

She showed her reluctance to agree to that. When she was leaving the office, she said, "Sorry for debating with you!"

I understood her attitude towards her job.

Some people say I have attitude - maybe I do... but I think you have to. You have to believe in yourself when no one else does - that makes you a winner right there.

Venus Williams

All the characteristics will originate because of the attitude of the person. A positive attitude causes a chain reaction of positive thoughts, events and outcomes. It is a catalyst and it sparks extraordinary results.

Wade Boggs

My attitude is that if you push me towards something that you think is a weakness, then I will turn that perceived weakness into a strength.

Michael Jordan

17

Stretch your world

When I decided to get into my new dream career, the speaking business, to become a professional motivational speaker, I recognized the strength zones in me. I knew what I was really good at and began to fine tune them, improving on the weak areas which I needed to recognize and develop within. I set up new routines and systems in my daily life. I tried to get up early, selected some books to read, determined to assimilate the contents thoroughly. I would watch YouTube videos related to motivation, and write down the important facts that the speakers emphasized in their speeches.

I reprogrammed my mind and tried to rewind my life. Many times in a day, I spoke to myself in the mirror, trying to practice some words and parts of my speeches, monitor my body postures and hand movements, and eye contact while talking. I assessed and ranked myself. Sometimes, I did quite well, and at other times, I got stuck in between the speech. I motivated myself, saying, "It's not necessary to be brilliant in the beginning; just start. Try to practice more, stick to your routine, and try to make a habit until the habit forms you."

Wherever I go, on roads or in shopping malls, till date, I do my practice, not too loudly. On many occasions, I noticed that people were looking at me, and when I turned back at them, I saw them laughing at me. I told myself, "Let them laugh and enjoy their lives. You practice and make your dream a reality."

I was firmly determined to keep on at this career without being distracted. I wanted to evolve into someone special and great in the process, and stay in this career until I die. I organized everything necessary to keep me in this speaking business, even hiring an employee to market and promote me. While practicing, I called my friend from Sri Lanka and recorded my videos. They were not up to the mark, as I was unwell and couldn't perform as expected. I hired a guy who created my website, and printed name cards and letterheads. I created a meet up group especially for contacts and networking. Announcing there that I was a motivational speaker, I shared with my well wishers the fact that my new career was going to start soon. I began to write a self help guide, this book, and told many friends that I was doing so. A few close friends said I was over reacting. Some things were to be kept secret until I really did something in public. But I deliberately did so to avoid going back once I had disclosed my private preparation to many. This was my challenge, one I had invested money and time in, and I had to do this. No excuses, no complaints, no one to blame! Only me! I had to practice, practice and practice.

Now I had to discipline and prove myself. I asked my employee to arrange a place to give a speech in before the year, 2015, ended. I didn't want to drag it out. A few months of preparation would suffice to initiate it, I guessed. I was ready to move even if I did make mistakes. I had no fear.

If you really want to start something, arrange the infrastructure, invest money and time, and make it public among friends. That way, you will be compelled to do it at any cost. Close down all the avenues and holes into which your mind can divert itself and sink into. Think about your start up, day and night, before sleep, and move forward even if it is hardly related to the same. This will provoke some hunches from your creative intelligence. Talk about your progress with your well wishers. Never with naysayers!

Regardless of where I live, I am a popular character in my circle. Even if it is a new place for me, within a few days, I get to know all the places in town where I can enjoy myself; all the drinking joints, spas and so on.

Earlier I used to eat up my time, drinking and chatting, rather than wholeheartedly focusing on my future, responsibilities and dreams. In my life, dreams had always been there, but they were not kicking and alive. I wanted to become someone special, but my actions towards that end were not sufficient. Over the last seven years, I even started something in a small way. I just about survived.

I trained my mind to relax, putting no pressure on it to analyze and process my thoughts. I preferred to give a shot to my body and mind through alcohol, after which I would wearily go to sleep. I tortured my body sometimes with excessive alcohol, sometimes with food. I destroyed my brain cells, reminding them of my failures, setbacks and disappointments. I failed to limit my past bitter experiences, along with my thinking and my words. My actions were mundane and boring. I didn't have the courage to override my habitual old fashioned style. I mourned, crying over my past.

For years my dreams were distracted, even as my new routines discouraged and distanced me from my circle. When close friends came to my place, I would talk about dreams, goals and affirmations, which bored them. They couldn't figure out my quick U turn and thought that I was going mad. They invited me to go out several times, and finally gave up coming to my place.

Only one guy kept coming over. Whenever he got the time, he would come and listen to me earnestly. He didn't speak English properly, and sometimes, he asked my employee to translate what I said into Hindi. After a month he came to me and happily declared that his business had grown to double its size. I keenly asked him how it had happened. He said that, following my instructions, he read his goal every day, did mind works and affirmations. He thanked me and left.

That was a turning point. I rushed to my office room, took out my goal book from the book shelf and read my goals. I told myself that I had to be a leader by example. From that day onwards, I would read my goals three times a day. As it had been proved, I told someone about the importance of goal reading every day, and he came up with results and figures. I was impressed.

I used to go to Ambience mall, Gurgaon, every day. I would sit for one or two hours every day at my favorite Starbucks, sipping hot coffee. Sometimes I would write. The noise of the place didn't disturb me or my thoughts. I heard that many writers preferred to be in calm, isolated places while writing. I was neither in the position, nor could I afford to go out of the city and engage in my writing in leisure. I enjoyed the crowd who came over. Usually I treated them with my contagious smile. The staff was curious to know what I was doing every day, spending time in this mall. Some assumed that I had a shop in the mall. Some thought that I was a rich guy and that it was better to keep contacts with me. I was always on their priority customer list. Sometimes they served my drink at my table and took the money later. I made many friends over there, as was my habit.

Taxi Driver

Whenever I went out of the main exit of the mall, a certain taxi driver called out to me every day. He smiled at me and said, "Sir, taxi." But I refused his offer with a smile. Every day this was a routine, "Sir, taxi." I always refused.

One day he added something to his offer. "Sir, taxi." I smiled as usual, and he added, "Today's my son's birthday."

That clicked in my mind. I also have a son. At times I had also struggled to afford his birthday gifts. I said, "Ok, let's go." I paid him a good tip. He was very happy. The next day, when I came out he was talking to another guy. I heard the conversation. He said that it was his birthday. He got the fare. I understood something. He made a constant effort in a creative way that didn't harm anyone. He tried to do his best. He always looked joyful! Enthusiastic! He attracted his goals.

Again one day, I got into his cab. He said, "Sir, I bought a new cab." This time, apart from the tip, I handed over to him my favorite affirmation which I carry wherever I go. It's for attracting wealth and success. I saw big hopes enlightening his face.

Avanti

There was a very nice car displayed in Ambience mall, Gurgaon. I thought it was imported from somewhere. Striking looks! Many people - young, old, male and female - went and took photos with the car without any hesitation! The Avanti car, costing 34 lakhs, had been made in India by an Indian designer.

One day I thought I would do a simple survey. I went to the people who were taking photographs and asked them some questions.

"Do you like this car?" One guy answered, "Yes, why not?"

"Are you planning to buy this car?" He said, "No!"

I asked him again, "I mean, not today. In the future?"

He said, "I can't say; if I can make money, yes."

I spoke to a young lady, "Will you buy this car one day?" She said, "No way. For us, the only chance is taking photos like this."

"Why, are you not sure about your future? You will not make enough money to buy this?"

"I don't think so!"

I talked to the middle aged executive who came there with his wife and children. I asked, "Will you bc able to buy this car?"

He said, "There are a lot of things to be done; in this life, no!"

I talked to the sales girls who were promoting the car there. "Will you buy this car one day, in the future?"

They laughed out loud and said, "If we get rich husbands!"

At least they had hopes about rich husbands. It was not bad and there were possibilities.

I spoke to more than ten people. I didn't get the answer that I expected from them. I thought someone would say enthusiastically, "Yes, of course. I dream to buy this and I surely will." Many people are not sure of what they really want in their lives. They measure their future according to who they are at present. Stuck with current income brackets, they don't believe in a possible change of life style and feasible achievements.

In India, the average life expectancy is 65–70. After retirement, many people age fast. Sri Lanka is no different. I believe that, except in Japan, China, Singapore and Malaysia, in all other Asian countries, there is not much of a difference. With advancing age, people let their dreams retire. Scientists have discovered that even in the nineties, the human brain will function more than in the thirties, if people are healthy. Unfortunately statistics give us a comfortable excuse to give up even the expectation of living till the nineties. When we live for 70 years, one third of life we sleep, and 12–16 years, we spend on education and training. Traveling and entertainment, also, take up much of our time. Approximately 16 years remain as productive years of our lives, which are very few to achieve great things in life. That is why we should release and maximize our talents in full, and to do so, we have to achieve optimal health and extend our life expectancy.

Many people enjoy things, but are too lazy to envision what they really want. They are not ready to stretch. By chance or by fortune, they would be content if they get something free. It's not their fault, as they have been trained to think in that way. We refer to them as common men and they are a majority in numbers.

I didn't get my photograph with that car, but I focused clearly and got a photograph of it in my mental eye. In my mind, I changed the color because the car displayed there was yellow. I didn't like it and so I made it red. I felt the happiness of owning that car, imagining that I had made a phone call to my son to say, "I bought this car." He said, "You are wonderful, papa, and your dreams are still alive." I got into the driving seat and drove it to the road. I noticed everybody was looking at the car as I parked it in front of my home. My son came running and took my photo while I was in the driving seat.

Free of cost, I envisioned it, with a detailed description. Today I would not buy it, but one day, surely! I went to my office and noted it down in my goal book.

I was happy to drive my red Avanti car by 31December 2016. I had set the criteria and standardized my goal.

Many people have dreams. Unless you set standardized goals with definite dates, it will remain just a dream. Also you have to follow the rule of consistency in what you are doing to accomplish your dream.

Memory count

1. Have huge dreams, set goals immediately and write them down to impress the subjective faculty of your mind. If you don't have goals with descriptions and deadlines, your dreams will remain fantasies. Don't hesitate to write goals due to a lack of resources needed to achieve your goals. They can be attracted any moment. Have faith; it is vital.
2. Find those abilities which can lead to competency and focus on them. Don't focus on your weaknesses. If you do so, you will waste time to even get to average standards. We will not live forever. Time is too short to waste. Strength zones will improve soon, and present impressively beautiful results. Sometimes even those you haven't imagined!
3. Sometimes you may love doing something which doesn't give you monetary rewards. Don't focus on them until you become well off enough to enjoy your hobbies.
4. Share the major thing that you are striving to achieve with your close circle. The repetition of those statements will rouse your energies and push them forward.
5. Add creativity in what you are doing. Even if it's a common thing that you are doing for a living, combine it with valuable ingredients like creativity, to get a unique shape and incredibly vast results, leading towards success.
6. Measure your progress. There is no other person to supervise you and issue reports about you, apart from you. Give marks to yourself. Don't underestimate your capacities.
7. Don't mention to anyone that you are a simple person who gets satisfied easily with the things that you have. Satisfaction means enough actions, according to the ancient Romans. Have you performed enough actions? Prove that you are worthy of deserving big results.
8. Show that you are a person who can take on any given responsibility. Be responsible when you rise or dip or when your organization does well or badly.

"Your life is the fruit of your own doing. You have no one to blame but yourself."

Joseph Campbell

9. Don't be self-centered because you have something big to achieve. Cast your bread upon the water. Allocate time for others.
10. Get cheer leaders to cheer you up even when you make a little progress. Parents, spouse, children or friends! Don't, however, let them overestimate you.
11. Encourage other dreamers to accomplish their goals, and respect their dreams as well. Don't downgrade or show their negative points, if you are not professional in their particular field.
12. Grounded practical plans are very important. So be realistic according your own measures, instead of the opinions of others.

18

Use the opportunity of today

Life is a progress, and not a station.

Ralph Waldo Emerson

I got up around 8 o'clock one day in winter, feeling quite lazy. But my dream kicked me out from the bed. I lived in a single bedroom with minimal facilities, which, in fact, was not a house for me when compared to my previous lifestyle, but only a transit point in my life's journey. I never lived there mentally. My physical body found that place to house it temporarily. In my mind I always lived in a mansion where my dream home was located.

I had my protein shake and vitamins quickly. It was in my priority list, because I wanted to maintain optimal health. Also the business which I was doing was associated with those wonderful products. When I started to use them, I saw a clear difference in my physical appearance.

I had a quick shower; luckily hot water was available. I dressed up nicely, and as I had some branded ties bought in Sri Lanka and Italy, I wore a Kenzo tie. I checked my pocket, found a few hundreds, which would be sufficient only for two coffees and transportation. I checked my metro card, and rushed downstairs from the top floor, using the stairs. It was good exercise for me. In my hand was a black leather bag with some literature and a note book, a Samsung tablet and a very old Nokia basic phone, concealed most of the time, in my pocket.

I walked up to the metro station because I didn't have much money to spend on three wheelers. While wearing a tie, it's better to walk, than go by public auto. India has three wheelers which can carry more people. We have to pay very little. I got into the metro, got down at Malviar Nagar metro station, and got into a shared auto to Select city walk. I stepped into Coffee bean, wearing my usual smile, and ordered my favorite Cappuccino. I sat comfortably, exhaling the worries and inhaling the fantasies I had. It was a place beautiful enough for me to admire.

I dreamt that, if the people who had fixed the meetings with me showed up, I would be able to develop my business soon, because they had something special in them. I had met them in the metro some time ago and shared my business idea with them. They were interested in starting something which would provide them a residual income. Moreover, they attended my phone calls, and when they missed my call, they called me back. Both worked in major corporations holding executive positions. Thus, they revealed signs which good prospective partners normally possess.

Two hours flew by. Nobody showed up as promised. Were the two scheduled meetings going to be cancelled? I was quite hesitant to call them again because that would go against me. If I overdid my interest, they would think that I had more benefits than them in this business. I got a little nervous. I kept smiling at visitors who came in to Coffee bean, sometimes standing up to shake their hands, and exchange cards. I tried to hide my disappointment, but kept checking my phone to see whether I had any missed calls from them. I checked my pocket again. Money was sufficient for only one more coffee. The little man in my heart tried to put me down. He said, "You talk about wealth creation, financial freedom, residual income, but you don't have anything which you are talking about," he chuckled.

"Wait, man, I am still on the way. In the process, you can't see my dream and vision. Today, I don't have money in my pocket, but you can't see the wealth in my invisible store. It's like a bank, and I am rich in my mind and thoughts. The only thing I have to do is transmute my thoughts into money." I went to the counter to order another coffee.

Ok, I had fuel for another three hours. I bought take away. It was time to roam around in the shopping mall and make cold contacts.

Again I smiled, smiling with my dream. Some people glanced at me strangely. Some didn't smile at all. Others asked, "Do you know me?" I moved forward. Noted down contacts! Tried to make friends with strangers! I told the little man in me, "Do you think that I am prospecting people for my business? No, I am building my dream."

Even if they didn't show up, it didn't matter. I still had the guts to pursue my dream. I had used my opportunity today in the maximum way. Those who didn't show up probably didn't have a larger vision. I worked for me. They worked for others. There had to be people to work for others also. Only if they were ready could I share my vision, and take them along my path with me. No reply from my little man! Darkness showed up, lights came on in the lampposts. Rejection had approached me and my heart had chased it away. I walked to the road and got into the shared auto.

We need to have a new release in our life every moment; a release of life like a new motion picture, a new song album, or a new book with excitement and thrill. Always think that the present day is a new release of life and use it fully without any delay and hesitation. At every moment in life, what can we release? Your brain will raise the question. We can release a new thought; thoughts are the things that build our house of life. The more thoughts you allow, and the more ideas that you create, and the more things of value will be produced. Don't empty your mind or procrastinate, doing zero value projects, but fill your mind with brand new ideas. Search for them from your mental eye, and close your eyes when you can't see solutions with your naked eyes. They will jump out from your creative faculty.

Always find what else remains to be done even if you are tired of experimenting with things, and your circumstances are not that good. Maybe you are broke, having failed not just once, but several times. Give a chance to your dream to bloom again. If you didn't have a big dream before, make it big now. In a minute, there will be a fresh start to your life. Maximizing the hours and days in your life, you can embrace every day with new expectations, and a new level of achievement, according to your wish, desire and hope.

The size of the activity you perform in a day is initially not important. Initiate new and creative thoughts, so that you can use your untouched valuable talents, not only in one segment, but in several fields, until you identify the firm area to be mastered to attract the top level of your expectation.

You all know that you are not going to live for more than a hundred years. Very rarely does someone live beyond that.

Divide your age into three parts. Over the first twenty years, you do not have 100% control over yourself. You are not mature enough to handle affairs and things alone. A few extraordinary characters can be found who took the responsibility for all their activities. Some have been successful as they are self-made. Between the ages of twenty and forty, many settle with the basic needs of life and live in their comfort zones, taking care of their job, marriage, house, car, school fees, parents' medical expenses, rent, insurance and the like. Career changes and promotions are the major basic needs that everyone hankers after.

From forty to sixty, few people try to do something different after experiencing many ups and downs in life. It is difficult to shift from your practices, but some conquer this difficulty. In the forties, you get a somewhat clear picture of life, which induces you to see and feel things differently. I jogged my memory and went back to that age, staying there for a while to understand the essentials of life's behavior and transition. After the forties, many people suffer from health problems. Firstly, an unhealthy life style can cause health issues. Diabetes, high blood pressure and obesity will guide you to hospitals. The second important issue is financial You will seek financial freedom issues, better retirement plans, residual income, your own business, freedom issues and more time for your family.

Fortunately, I failed before the age of forty. When I was 37, I was broke. So I got a clear understanding of my life and my actions before forty, and tried to find solutions until I was forty two. Now I know what to master in my life to go towards success by accomplishing my dream. But if I could undo things in my life, I would go back to the age of 26, when I completed my academic and professional qualifications, and start from scratch. Enough time is there due to my good personal and health development schemes. But I still regret that I wasted 26 years. This is not to discourage anyone in their middle and old ages. However, it is better if you are below thirty, to be able to understand the truth and the circumstances of life at different ages, which will enable you to change your life accordingly. Because the sooner you do so, the better!

Maybe many opportunities come your way in life, but you haven't taken them into account as opportunities. You fear they are coming to divert your goals and waste your time. You have to be a man of opportunities. When they walk beside you, you have to jump and grab them. Sometimes opportunities come as ideas. You neglect to write them down on paper to be considered later, as you are busy with your job or small business, enjoying life within your comfort zone until you lose the comfort, not only for you, but for your children and family too. While living, it is always a boon to have back up plans.

Some ladies find opportunities suddenly, when they lose their pillars in life, maybe when their husbands lost their jobs or suddenly when they say bye to them. Until such a situation arises, you chase away your opportunities with confidence. Not that dependability is bad, but having a plan B is always worth it.

Many ideas jostle about in my mental drawer which has still not been unfolded. I am working on writing a book that I could have finished ten years back. I postponed my life of luxury by ten years. I could have started my speaking career at least three years back. In a nutshell, I postponed my future by years. That is why I am emphasizing the importance of this moment, this hour, today. It is yours. Don't let anyone to pour out their opinions on you and tarnish your today. It belongs to you, along with your right and obligation to change yourself, and live life in full to make changes in the masses.

"Sometimes we feel that one individual's action is very insignificant. Then we think, of course, that the effect should come from channeling or from a unifying movement. But the movement of the society, a community or a group of people means joining individuals. Society means the collection of individuals, so the initiative must come from individuals. Unless each individual develops a sense of responsibility, the whole community cannot move. Therefore, it is very essential that we should not feel that individual effort means less. You should not feel that way. We should make an effort."

Dalai Lama

If you want to make a young world with healthy living beings, who stay rich and enjoy real values in life, by guiding and directing your next generations towards prosperity, begin to think today itself. How many think about simple things which make a major difference on the life and impact on this planet? Peace, love and happiness! Do you envisage the peace which your future generations can enjoy in this world? If there is no peace, will there be love? If there is no love, will there be any happiness? Why are we so self - centered as to depart from this life, only leaving material values, properties or money for our future generation to take care of themselves. If they also think similarly, who will take the initiative to bring about some radical mind campaigns to change the mindsets of people? Why do most of us not attempt to reform people's minds according to their capacity, thus, fulfilling the responsibility which lies in them?

There was an era of my life, when I made use of my day and opportunities in a highly effective manner. It was no fun, and really arduous. However, the skills and the talents that I honed then helped me to drive and overcome tougher fields in life.

Memory count

1. Maximize your days, make use of opportunities today. Don't let your mind postpone your prioritized task for tomorrow. Search for new arrivals in your mind, stretch your mind and bring forth fresh and novel ideas and concepts to present to your future.

2. Your brain muscles also need exercise like your body muscles. If you are curious and question how you can attain your expected levels every day, with time to focus, your mind will perk up with solutions. Give adequate rest to your mind and recharge your mind energy, instead of working for a whole day like a machine and getting exhausted. When you are exhausted, your performance will not be up to the mark.
3. Sometimes our mind needs emotional bribes; romance and sex, new clothes, different cuisines, movies, a glass of wine, good friends or a vacation. Don't be a robot. Live life king-size!
4. Don't let opportunities slip away and evade you; respect, greet and embrace them once they appear. Big opportunities come with a bag full of obstacles. Sometimes only the hardware is visible, but the software will make it easy when you apply it in the process.
5. Don't waste your youth and wait until adversities flow over your head. Learn from universal experiences and avoid mistakes as much as possible.
6. Practice and build your intuitive power. Sense all the vital things that are going to come your way, in your personal, professional and spiritual life, and that of others close to you. It's hard if you don't own natural intuition, but you can acquire and hone it.
7. Don't wait for others to open the doors to your fortune. Pigs never dig for others. Take the initiative to shift if you really need to. Even if others don't save you in your grief, if you are in position to help them, do so without expecting gratitude.
8. Use your available sources to the maximum. You never know what the catch point is. When you use all, one will surely work out. It can be your knowledge or talent, or your characteristics, your dress, your pleasant smile or looks, contacts or relations. Try everything out without shrinking.
9. Carry your vision code. Prove that you are a great visionary who can help others to see. When rejection and failure strike, shield them from your vision, like a great warrior who shields himself from the arrows of enemies.
10. You are living with people in society. Others may do better than you at present and you may feel you are slow. While many survive well, only a few thrive well. Don't get discouraged or compete for others'

accounts. Focus on your bank. Day by day, add values. Your efforts will be converted into royalty one day.

11. Always think that you have been given a responsibility to become a better transformer and prove your worth. The world needs many creative performers in every field. Be number one in your selected field.
12. Do the right thing to deliver the maximum benefit to others too. You will be rewarded too. When you go to battle, don't go alone; accompany your soldiers and look after them after the war.

The Lord rewarded me according to my righteousness; according to the cleanness of my hands he has recompensed me.

2 Samuel 22:21

Do something that has legitimate and moral values, as it will lift your self-esteem. You can be sure to receive material rewards and intangible rewards.

19

What motivates you?

Desire is the key to motivation, but it's determination and commitment to an unrelenting pursuit of your goal - a commitment to excellence - that will enable you to attain the success you seek.

Mario Andretti

When I was in school, the new books given by the government motivated me to go to school. Not only me, but many students who remained absent on other days, were present, eager to receive new books. I can still smell the fragrance which came from those new books.

When we get new uniforms or new clothes from our parents in the beginning of the new term, we get motivated to go to school without making excuses. When our team wins, when we get good marks, when we shine in debates, when our drama is selected to the next level, and when our teachers appreciate us, we get motivation to do things even better than before. These are simple examples that most of us have experienced. There are many times when my hair cut, facial, new dress and perfume motivate me to go out in public, meet people and hold meetings confidently.

When we get jobs, initially the salary and incentives motivate us, followed by the working environment. If it is cool, we feel motivated to stay; if it is unhealthy, it motivates us to leave. When we grow and have kids and family, those loved ones motivate us to do something to fulfill their aspirations. At other times, your society, and even your responsibility towards your country as a responsible citizen, will act as a boost to motivate you.

One time when Sri Lanka was in the midst of a serious war with the rebels who asked for a separate state in the country, one army soldier made history by sacrificing his life to save thousands of lives in the camp. Rebels were moving towards the camp, there were no options, and a huge disaster was going to happen. This soldier jumped into the rebel's tank with bombs and killed himself, destroying the rebel tank. He, thus, prevented the rebel tank which carried sophisticated weapons that could kill all his fellow soldiers, from entering the camp. His responsibility and strong love for his country motivated him to act heroically.

A motive to act, reason and desire keeps you motivated. The important thing is to keep you motivated enough to retain a big fire within yourself. A small fire gives little heat and a big fire will give big heat with a big impact. If you really want do something big and significant in your life, you have to have strong, compelling reasons that motivate you to accomplish that. Even to survive in life without doing anything extraordinary you need motivation of a kind.

At times very minor obstacles, problems and issues come across as major things, merely due to a lack of big dreams and vision. If you dwell in big dreams, you will never focus on the processes to be passed to achieve those dreams, because you expect glitches, barriers and blocks. Apart from physical blocks, sometimes, a block within our mind, keeps us from moving forward. We feel lost on the roads. Even people with high levels of energy, spirit and enthusiasm feel so at times. I too have experienced this on many occasions. There are numerous responsibilities and actions to be taken to see my dream as a monetary and physical equivalent. However, some unexpected distractions appear. Now I expect them and they distract me for a while, one or two days maximum. After that transit period, I again begin to move. Today I understand the importance of doing something, even if it is small in size, towards my destination.

The time that I take today is quite long to accomplish my outcome. But if I keep on with the effort and practice without letting my fire die, I will surely reach my winning post. The rules of Success apply to everyone and people who utilize them get the results, a fact proven by many individuals from humble backgrounds, with no money and no college degrees.

I want to constantly hold my head up and keep myself fully charged. In order to sustain the heat in me, I have to connect with chargers, characters and people who have big hopes for my future and push me to accomplish them. If I am to make my son, mum, loved ones and well -wishers happy, inspire my people and make my country proud, I still have to do many things to achieve.

Having been out of my country for ages, I can only connect with my son and mum over the phone, Viber and Skype. It alarms me since I wish to do something significant in their lives. If I cannot contact them for a day or two, my energy level instantaneously plummets, slowing me down. When

I chat next with them, my energy level gets a boost. My loved ones have an amazing remote control over me.

Sometimes my friends contact me on Facebook, suggesting that this is the right time for me to be in politics. Even if they are just simple and light opinions, they serve as a sort of appetizer that stimulates me to have my main course. It is amazing to discover that someone has hopes in you, having noticed your talents and capabilities. When we are mentally low, these hopes work as helpful enhancers, and dream building tools. Sometimes you may not feel worthy about yourself, but others do. These people nourish, and put water and fertilizer to help your seed plant to grow. Hang around and keep in contact with these people who play significant roles in your life. Sometimes, when you do not believe in or trust yourself, others do. They strengthen your level of confidence. Avoid people who have a low opinion about you, and when you bump into them, cut short your time with them. If they pour out something to demotivate you, without any delay, override those negative energies with positive ones, by calling your loved ones or well - wishers over the phone or listening to the favorite tape of your mentor.

When I started to practice, I made some important preparations to begin my new career as a motivational speaker and writer. I had no clue of what I was going to speak or what I was going to write when I sat in my room. My private hunches emerged, making me ponder over how to start. It needed a lot of sacrifice. I had to sacrifice who I was, in order to turn myself round, stand on my feet and raise my head in front of the crowd again.

I cannot hang around with losers. I can't entertain the word 'can't'. Remaining in the zone of temporary illusions without an obsession to drive is insane. It is vital to avoid less civilized and less worthy things to avoid low self-esteem. Without an invitation, some friends come over to try and kill time. They have no idea what I am up to. When I try to strictly follow my routine, it becomes worse. Some come seeking opinions and open their emotional taps, and I can't chase them away easily. What I do at such times is to use them as an opportunity to share my vision and keep alive my dreams. I use my newly learned words to explain and illustrate things with my newly created stories and true life sagas.

What is tougher is going out with them. They are not my enemies, but the enemy within me gets energized from my circle, and finds ways to be at leisure. Sometimes I get a call from the spa while I'm writing.

It is very relaxing and tempting to lie on the spa bed while a beautiful girl's soft fingers touch my body. This makes it tough to stick to my practice plan while reading and listening to tapes. I may be a grown man, but sometimes maturity lies only in my body and appearance. Mentally I become a kid, sometimes a teenager who does things without thinking too much; sometimes I feel that I am in my twenties, an age when I can't control myself from doing risky things and taking radical steps. I abstain from forcefully disciplining myself, but understand its importance in my constant efforts. I do things on my own, being my own boss, without even a coach. All I have is an unseen dream and unacquainted feelings within my imagination to become a highly paid motivational speaker, bestselling author and entrepreneur. I have my mentor and idol in my mind. However, I have not seen or met them, face to face.

I considered using a computer to write my book, but it was troublesome work. My fingers couldn't find letters in the beginning, and I didn't know how to use both my hands. I have seen people typing very fast. I felt that I wouldn't be able to reach that level, because I couldn't type fast. It took me one month to come up to quite a good speed. Now I enjoy writing on a PC more than writing by pen, the advantage being that it is easy to read again, correct and edit. Until you do something that you have not experienced before, you can't really feel the real nature of that particular thing.

If you want to be somewhere you have never been, or do something you have never done, cursory efforts and an ordinary desire towards that is not sufficient. You have to act, learn something, gain some skill, and make some changes in your life in a visible and noticeable way, not only for you, but for others too.

Initially I wrote around five pages and I thought I could stick to that every day. Some days it went down to one page as my mind went blank. On other days, I could write nothing. But what was important was that I had begun something that kept me motivated most of the time. Since I had started writing my book, having announced it to my close circle and regular friends, I had to move forward. I couldn't stop.

Sometimes I talk to myself and say, "This time you have done something laudable. No excuses can be made. Your self-development gives you fruits. No one and no circumstance can block you. Now you must do it. You have to launch your book soon. It will be a marketing tool for your speaking career in future."

One of my friends started a project with me, a good example to illustrate the above. He has a family, with school going children. He starts things interestingly but never finishes them. Sometimes, he explains the reasons for his inactions, and the excuses that make him slow. He is unhappy with his wife, whom he doesn't like. This is a good reason that makes him neutral and he validates it by revealing her mistakes.

When he came to our office, most of the time he showed little energy, and instead, talked about his bitter experiences and past incidents. In the beginning, I didn't want to hurt his feelings, but I signaled to him that I didn't want to pay attention to personal issues that could be managed by him. But until I explained this verbally, he missed my signals too.

He would come to office most of the time on an empty stomach and didn't show an interest in eating. He didn't drink water much and hardly went to the wash room. Later, when I recruited another employee, he started his negative campaign to share his life stories with her and wasted our productive time. He claimed that he didn't need motivation, for, according to him, he was self motivated. I asked myself. In what way was he self motivated? Was it for inaction?

I was tense, having realized I had made a mistake in starting a partnership with this neutral character. When I gave him time to complete some work with reasonable deadlines, he failed to do that, not once, but three times. I wanted to end the partnership that I had spent my money and time on, to avoid further losses. He wished to attain success, but was averse to change, because he didn't see any compelling reasons to act and to be motivated, whether over money or other achievements in life.

Success is a science and it doesn't respond to just wishes or wants. You have to apply the laws of success applied by superior people, who have attained their respective high levels. Again my heart reconfirmed the validation of a strong will, in producing things from thoughts and impulses.

Memory count

1. Have reasons for actions, not for inaction. Reasons for inaction are excuses to postpone your success.
2. Even small things can motivate you, if you take them as motives to act. Build motivation through small things and spread them throughout life.
3. Don't take minor obstacles as major problems. In the process of achieving anything remarkable, you will surely confront problems.

4. Sometimes you will not believe in yourself, but if others do, they are important characters to rally around you.
5. Have space in your heart to listen and let the emotions of others flow. Make them comfortable, but don't be a slave to your emotions and let them override your main objectives.

No matter how good you are at planning, the pressure never goes away. So I don't fight it. I feed off it. I turn pressure into motivation to do my best.

Benjamin Carson

Wanting something is not enough. You must hunger for it. Your motivation must be absolutely compelling in order to overcome the obstacles that will invariably come your way.

Les Brown

There's always the motivation of wanting to win. Everybody has that. But a champion needs, in his attitude, a motivation above and beyond winning.

Pat Riley

People need motivation to do anything. I don't think human beings learn anything without desperation.

Jim Carrey

20

Work Whole Heartedly

No matter what we pursue, we have to do it with our heart; not half -heartedly, but whole heartedly. Many of us do not use our potential, unaware of the potentiality which we hold within. In fact, if we use all our potential, a life time would not be sufficient to accomplish the outcome. The important thing is to release and maximize our potential until it results in excellence.

We take pride when someone brings victory or medals to our country. Have you ever thought of the efforts behind that? When you see a huge six stroke by the batsman, how cheerful you are! Have you ever noticed the tearful background behind that, or the hardships he underwent in his life, the efforts he took to qualify to play the national game, the practice he did, and the sacrifices he made in private? People who are awarded and rewarded in public do much hard work and practice in private.

When you see athletes with amazing fitness or the six packs of sportspersons, you do not see the practice, persistence and perseverance behind those muscles. You don't see the pain, or the hardships they underwent.

Bulbs give you light to chase away darkness, but you can't imagine the dark side Thomas Alva Edison underwent when he was struggling with his experiments.

If you do something whole heartedly, you will see the progress, day by day, and step by step, sometimes exceedingly and abundantly. Progress will certainly involve risk; mainly the risk of losing your comfort zone, moving away from bad relations, leaving you temporarily in isolation, keeping away from delicious sweet dishes, your favorite wine, logging out of your Facebook account, turning off your best series, risking your long hours of sleep and the like.

Learning new skills, starting new ventures, writing a book, preparing for a speech, losing weight, conquering a critical illness and most importantly, adjusting with your life partner; in all these, whole hearted efforts are necessary. In the process, you will have to build mental or physical assets which determine your success.

Self mastery is the key to open the gate of glory even if you have failed in most of your attempts. Always remember; you should try to major in one branch of the subject which you are following, or intend to follow in future. Don't just wait, day dream and share ideas with people that you are going to do something with, people who do not encourage you. Don't expect their feedback. In fact, their negative opinions will obstruct your start.

Try to initiate. You may not be great initially, but your initiative will surely activate your talents. While doing something, despite making mistakes, you have to have the courage not to commit those mistakes again, having learned through your own past experience or those of others. If you read a good book which contains the success stories of super successful people, you can save five years of your life, avoiding mistakes and failures. You can attend to seminars and workshops which give you inspirational messages through their life stories, and the tools and techniques they use. You can avoid a series of failures and drive towards success. If the ground where you are positioned is not suitable for you, you have to move somewhere else, and initiate your plans in a new turf that will bring you victory.

When Honda was rejected by Toyota, Japan, he went to USA to start his business. Never be the victim of a big fish, until you grow mature enough to fight back. Grow, improve and develop nonstop, until success embraces you. You don't need to chase success. If you are ready to accept it, success will come after you. Arm yourself with qualifications and prove that you are the most suitable one to align with. Of course, it takes considerable time. Even five years or ten years are acceptable, and if it is finance, you can expect to get financial freedom, residual or royalty type of income. I took finance as an example, as, even if it is not everything in life, many things will follow behind it. To become a professional in a particular field takes time.

The next time you feel motivation, note down something that you love to do; lose weight, maybe. Many people don't like a body structure that does not fit well in their clothes. Unbearable weight and ugly looking bellies trouble your mind when you stand in front of the mirror. In the work place, you will not perform well, but feel sleepy and lethargic. If you sit somewhere, you will not want to get up. I have experienced a similar kind of embarrassing situation before. Write a book, become a speaker or singer, play an instrument, have a fulfilling relationship, start an independent business and create wealth, and become a star in any preferred field. If you accomplish the thing which you want to achieve, feel the happiness assuming that it were already done. It is worthy to have something big to stretch your capacity. After writing down the thing that you want to achieve, start some action to make that dream real. Don't do something lofty or adventurous in the beginning. I began many things in my life in a brilliant way, yet couldn't maintain them for long, and ended up becoming mediocre.

What you can't get out of, get into wholeheartedly.

Mignon McLaughlin

I think when you move past your fear and you go after your dreams wholeheartedly, you become free.

LL Cool J

I like to dedicate myself wholeheartedly to a cause so that I have more impact. My goal is to shed light on the beauty of the ocean and how important it is for our planet.

Hayden Panettiere

What we must try to be, of course, is ourselves and wholeheartedly. We must find out what we really are and what we really want.

Nelson Boswell

When you go into projects, you can't look at it as limited; you have to dive into it wholeheartedly to be true to the writer's vision.

Jolene Purdy

21

Are you pretending or attending?

Pretending that we live doesn't make us alive.

Serj Tankian

Pretending is common in every part of the society. It is an illusive thing that initially misguides others, and at last, turns out to be a pretender. People who pretend are not serious characters, and not having developed their mindset, they will never amount to much in their lives. Not only individuals, but also some countries, pretend in many things, specially their economic and military capacity, disclosing false data. They want to impress others and it is only a temporary attempt that covers the reality. Governments also pretend to do well to keep their respective party voters unchanged.

How many people invest time to master their strength zones, instead of wasting time on their weak zones? Many have no idea about what they are pursuing, as their landing positions are not clear. They waste time focusing on what they are really not good at. When you follow something that you are weak at, you will be incompetent. First find the field that you can be competent in. Even though the skills in each and every area are learnable, be smart enough to chose the most result oriented thing that can be learned, and acquire specialized knowledge in a shorter time span. Time should be used productively.

Many students want to become doctors and engineers, but people who are not good at math, face many struggles and get disappointed, and fail or settle for lower positions in the same field. They pretend to follow something worthwhile to impress others, but they end up in depression. Sometimes, parents want to impress relatives and neighbors by boasting that their children are doing well in fields they are actually not good at.

I was not good at math, in fact, I was very weak. I could hardly reach fifty percent. I realized that I would not be able to be an engineer. I was good at the arts subjects and I chose them and got through the exams. But many of my family members, my cousin sisters and brothers, didn't admit their weak zones unfortunately, and tried desperately, only to get poor results.

I met many people at different ages of my life, while I was in politics and pursuing the network marketing business. Many people told me that they didn't have anything to prove. They were done, and content with their lives. In fact, some had more properties than one, some had finance in banks, and so they had fulfilling careers, according to them. They didn't want to stretch or do something extraordinary for themselves and for the society. They didn't want to even think about it because they were complacent in their comfort zones. They thought that they were born to do what they did. Not that I am complaining! Everybody cannot do something significant. But if they did what they were capable of doing, rather than what they normally did, it would help them to reach remarkably high levels in society.

I met a person who had a factory and was doing very well, having millions of money. He was in his sixties and he said he didn't have anything to achieve in his life. I told him money had given him options. "Why don't you think about optimum health and follow a good health plan?" He said, "Everybody dies one day. No need to live forever!"

That is true but nobody would ready be to die right away, even if they did go to heaven after that.

It is better to enjoy a healthy life. Show others that you have achieved a healthy life style and a disease free life, and encourage them to stick to that kind of life style. It will give you happiness and inner gratification. You can do some volunteer service to the community, state or country. It will heighten your zest of living and also increase your life expectancy.

Hypocrisy is not a way of getting back to the moral high ground. Pretending you're moral, saying you're moral is not the same as acting morally.

Alan Dershowitz

People are sad. People are broke. People are worried about money, people are worried that they're not enough and not amounting to anything and they don't feel good about themselves. People have rough times, and everybody's pretending it's not true, and we need to break that veneer.

Eve Ensler

I write from my soul. This is the reason that critics don't hurt me, because it is me. If it was not me, if I was pretending to be someone else, then this could unbalance my world, but I know who I am.

Paulo Coelho

That is a strange phenomenon, people pretending to be other people.

Andy Samberg

How you accept, evaluate and appreciate you, is what will decide the size of your achievement.

Keerthisinghe

22

Don't change the shape when circumstances and situations appear

If any of you lacks wisdom, you should ask God, who gives generously to all without finding fault, and it will be given to you.

James 1:5

One morning in 2007, (I do not recall the date and the month that the incident occurred), I was waiting near the back entrance of the 'Temple Trees', the then official residence of the president of Sri Lanka, located in the high security zone of Colombo, the capital. I was alone, with no body guards. The situation had changed so fast. There was no one to open the door of my car, to carry my mobile, or to escort me. I had been waiting for the arrival of one of the ministers of the government. In fact, he was my counterpart. I represented a constituency from my party, and the above mentioned minister of the government represented the same constituency from his party. I was a very big threat to him politically.

Once I took over the constituency in the very first presidential election, I set out to organize the constituency, and was able to bring down the margin of defeat from ten thousand to four thousand votes. This proved to be a headache to this powerful minister, who was very close to the then president. He did a lot of welfare activities to please the voters of the area. I waited for more than thirty minutes. I didn't have my own vehicle at that moment and all my cars and jeeps had already been sold to pay off a portion of the debts I had. Having incurred a large loss of money due to the presidential election expenses, I couldn't pay them off fully, even after three years.

The minister came with his Squad and asked me to get into his vehicle. I never thought of being associated with my political enemy. But circumstances and situations had pushed me to do so. Looking at him,

I said to myself, "Why are you doing this? You are going to adjust with your circumstances and situation. Look at him in comparison to you. What does he have? Does he have a good personality like you, an educational back ground; is he an orator like you, does he participate in debates in TV channels like you? Nothing! In comparison to you, he is nothing. His only plus point is that he became a minister in the ruling party." My heart asked me, "Why are you going to sacrifice your future? It's not easy to come back. Will they give you the proper position you deserve after this crossover? How can you trust them?"

This political marriage had been planned one day before I went to Temple Trees to a friend's house. A well connected businessman, he had joined hands with me in the last presidential election campaign. He had also been assigned to organize party events in our district. I trusted him and it was he who had arranged my party crossover through this minister.

We reached the security check point. Even though he was a minister, we underwent heavy security check up.

At the lobby, more than two hundred people were waiting to meet the president who was in another meeting. Almost two hours passed. The Minister was with me and he was happily introducing me to his fellow ministers and friends. One said to him, "What a huge relief! Now no one is there to challenge you." I was in the camp of my political enemies, and I had started regretting my decision. I told the minister that I would come back the next day, if the president was going to take more time. Reluctant to lose face, he urged me not to do that. He had already informed the president that I was present, and that at any moment, he would arrive. He suggested I should talk to the press before the president came. I disagreed as I wanted to get a proper assurance from the president about what I would get. However, the minister told me not to worry as he would look after everything. I had to trust him but I rejected his proposal to address the press before meeting the president.

Again I was isolated in my own mental world. My mind counseled me, "When circumstances and situations appear, you have to face and encounter them. Even before you started your political career, you should have anticipated the incoming problems and struggles. Now what you are doing is against the principles of success. You are going to compromise your dream for a temporary situation. You accepted and expected good results. When misfortune appears, you search for short cuts. It's not worth it and not the quality of a winner. There are many things to change in your life before you change your party. Have you thought about this?"

"How are you, Keerthi? Very happy to see you! We have many things to do in your area." The President came in with his usual cunning smile, greeting me before I greeted him. He talked with me around five minutes and said, "We will leisurely meet and discuss further things." He got a photograph taken with me.

The Press was waiting for me in another room and I addressed them. This was one of the major mistakes I committed in my life, and it took three - four months for me to realize the consequences.

The second time I met the president at the same place - Temple Trees. He was surprised about the posts which I held in my party, especially since I was a member of the economic affairs committee, which consisted of three members. I was the only member who didn't represent parliament. He was upbeat about the TV interview that I had participated in after joining him.

He called the chairman of the government TV channel and asked him to make me participate in TV programs continuously. He requested the secretary of the finance ministry to give me a good post. He talked on terrorist issues and the support extended by Iran. He also mentioned that he wanted to remove one of the young politicians in my area and put me in his place. He talked about things regarding hatred in which he showed his immaturity. My heart said that this man was not mature enough to become president of our country and I regretted my decision to join hands with him. However, I couldn't change the circumstances.

I tried to change the circumstances and the situation I faced, but they prevailed as they were. My finances were dismal, and my properties were for sale. One by one, they were sold as I strove to pay off all the debts I had. The situation became worse as I rued the silly mistake in my life. I had had so many other options, rather than joining the government party. My stance regarding the terrorist problem in the country was correct. I believed that it could be eradicated through war. This was the one issue that had tempted me to join the government.

But my party believed in the political solution. My position and economic situation didn't change, as promised by the minister, as I was not given any vital position in the government. In the dirty political game played by them, I was used by them and became a political victim. My friend, who had made the arrangements to coordinate with the minister, was helpless. I became more confused about myself and the situation than before. Today I rejoice that I was not given the position to be a part of the team of the said president, who lost in the recently held presidential election before completing his second term. The president and the majority of his stalwart ministers, are facing huge corruption charges and frequenting courts, presidential commissions and remand custody.

From time to time, I recall this incident. Recently I understood why I couldn't have taken a better and timelier decision. I didn't search for the invisible help coming from God. Instead, I believed and trusted in the visible support from humans. When we lose our mental equilibrium, human understanding provides limited support. I failed to deliver my circumstances and situations to God, who has total control of everyone and everything. When we don't connect with God for His counsel, a decision may go wrong. I believed in mere human powers that were too limited to encounter unexpected situations. I believed in others, not in myself, because I was shattered, mentally and emotionally, unwilling to listen to my heart and intuition. I didn't have the courage. I unconsciously disregarded the fortune I possessed, failing to understand the miracle working power within my inner strengths. The results brought me shame and disappointment, anger and vengeful thoughts.

I hadn't expected incredibly difficult problems in life that I couldn't cope with alone. I couldn't think clearly, or patiently wait until the situation had passed by. The way out loomed ahead, but I couldn't visualize it through the screen of my overwhelming problems. I was alone due to a lack of knowledge of God and His plans. I lost hope. Every decision I took added fuel to the fire. Finally I gave up and postponed my victory, turning my face against all the efforts which I had made in my journey.

The second reason was that I didn't pay attention to my inner capacities, and my creative intelligence. I had no idea about the power of the mind. Over the years, I have developed many things within me in my life which I wasn't aware of in my previous adverse situations.

Memory count

1. Expect bright things always and don't forget that certain circumstances and situations will appear to slow you down. Don't consider them as direction changers. They will stretch you and make you strong if you push forward. Do bear the bitter tortures that life hands you in the present, to enjoy sweet memorable experiences in the future. Send your dream forces to the war front and urge them to fight with the enemy called circumstances and situations.

In this battle, your giant dream will surely win. If you are beaten badly, temporarily retreat and give up the land, but don't give up your interest. Plan secretly, practice until the time comes, and train well. I do the same and accumulate all the required forces which will give me an advantage in the next fight.

2. When circumstances and situations keep things on hold for a while, think clearly and design a plan to troubleshoot them. Don't panic.
3. Always have back up plans, especially a plan B in your life. If plan A is struggling or underperforming, spend more time on B. Try to minimize the damage caused by A. Having plan B doesn't mean that you are not confident enough to pursue one purpose single-mindedly. More is always better, and so retain many sources until you turn strong.
4. Don't divert or get distracted from your dreams and goals. Despite the many difficulties you face, focus on the ultimate accomplishments, and bear current discomforts, after tightening your belts.
5. Adversities may be disguised blessings. You may not realize that when you undergo them. Be still.
6. Don't quit easily, and make excuses, as it will be almost impossible to bounce back. Also others, who were behind you, will establish their positions through perseverance. This is applicable to any industry or field.
7. Trust yourself when limiting forces appear, and affirm that, "I am always prospering." Strive to build your self confidence again to regain more than you lost earlier.
8. Seek God's counsel and expert advice in the field you are active in. Before taking any crucial decision, consult your heart and intuition. Until you are relaxed, don't give any commitment, make any vital decision or sign agreements.
9. Have loved ones behind your compelling desire, and imagine the results that your ultimate accomplishment will bring to change their lives. Then you will muster enough courage to confront adverse circumstances and situations.
10. Even though circumstances take away all your materials, money, resources, name and reputation, focus on your dream and strengthen your faith until your confidence reaches peak level. Once the storms are over, you will stand again like a huge rock. It may take a little or more

time, according to the size of the damage. But stick to the hope that it surely will. It's agonizing when adversities influence your belongings, but remaining in the game is the utmost quality and test of a winner.

11. Dream stealers will come like angels in disguise, with moderate plans to sweep you out from the field. You may not be able to figure out what's going on. In the above mentioned story, the same thing happened to me. Remember people who distract you, or divert your attention, will not have the moral bonds to protect you. Sometime they will laugh secretly and enjoy cruel happiness when you are helpless and in a dilemma.
12. Positive possibilities and constructive forces will stand parallel to destructive negative situations. If you are confused, you may miss the good ones, and instead, experience anguish over the bad things that happened to you. Relax and seek the answers from God.

7"Ask, and it will be given to you; seek, and you will find; knock, and it will be opened to you.

8"For everyone who asks receives, and he who seeks finds, and to him who knocks it will be opened.

Matthew7:7–8

In other words, if you constantly ask for, seek and knock at your creative intelligence, you will be rewarded with the expected results. Your creative faculty, which is within your reach, has an enormous and unlimited supply of all. Your subconscious mind is the creator of all your physical and mental assets.

Changing life is a change of character. If you build characteristics, transformation will be initiated instinctively.

Keerthisinghe

23

How to qualify yourself as a Winner

Many people have reasons and excuses for inaction, not the reasons for actions; or they neglect them.

Keerthisinghe

Once I commanded my mind to give me reasons as to why I couldn't complete things that I had started in my life on several occasions. Today I understand that my priority was different. It spelt 'can not', and not 'can'. I found some reasons for my inaction. I would console my mind with a sigh of relief, instead of allocating time to re-evaluate my failures. What I had really wanted in life was refreshed by irrational lousy thoughts. I got to know that sometimes, people around me were harsh critics, who said, "Look at him… being a lawyer, having so many talents; what is he doing?"

When I was doing business, I thought that I could have done better if I had possessed an MBA from a recognized foreign university. Focus was the one thing which I didn't have. I complained to myself but made no effort to acquire the degree. I thought if my parents were rich, I could have done something better than that I had pursued. I thought if I had supportive people around me, I could have done better. Expecting constant support from others, I didn't urge myself to grow with better thought patterns.

Of course, if I had had all the above mentioned things, it would have given me a better advantage, but they are not decisive factors in the achieving of success. People who had everything in life have failed, and people with nothing have won acclaim in their lives. Many billionaires today have transformed their lives from rags to riches. What I didn't understand was the importance of what I had in hand. I failed to realize what was inside me and make strategic plans based on that, to win in life. This caused me to experience several failures and missed opportunities in my young age.

I did my university entrance education in a rural college, which didn't have proper facilities, or even teachers to cover the syllabi. I studied two subjects without teachers, depending on some course guides. I didn't have a bicycle to go to school and walked three miles every day. When I walked back from school, the sun tortured me, emitting its scorching light. In the beginning, it was tough as I was not used to it, but after some days, it became a habit. I enjoyed it, and many students joined me on the way to school, even as many others passed me in their vehicles.

I was the only student who got selected to the university from my school that year. At the time, my focus was to enter university anyhow, so I tolerated all the hardships, because if I had allowed 'can't' to overcome me, I would have lost that opportunity too.

At the conclusion of the recently held presidential election, my friends and colleagues became ministers of the government and they were given significant portfolios. My relatives and some friends called me to say, "You missed the opportunity that you deserved." They were filled with regrets, but I was not. The reason was that my vision had expanded. Today, I can see no limits, and I live in a world with great expectations, believing that enormous possibilities are yet to appear before me.

Recently I got a phone call from my friend living in Milan. Her voice was shaking and she seemed distraught. She spoke around two minutes nonstop. "Can you send me soon to New Zealand or UK with my son? I can't live here with this man. He tortures and insults me all the time."

I asked, "How many years have you been in this marriage?"

She said, "Seventeen years."

"Can you wait seventeen minutes more?"

She laughed nervously.

I said, "Wait and listen carefully. I understand your situation, and will do something. At the moment, let us talk about how we can cope with this situation. Why do you think you were born here?"

She said, "I don't know! That is a question I have."

"You think that it was an accident? No, no, it's not. God had a purpose when he created you," I said. "Why are you living?"

"Because I was born."

"Do you have any reason to live this life, any compelling reason?"

"Yes! My son."

"Ok, good! Then you have a definite purpose in life and a burning reason to live. You have to organize your activities around them. You can't panic, make excuses or complain about anything or anyone. It's you who have the right to take decisions. Be patient, make yourself disciplined and don't let your situations shake your mental stamina. Be still and plan; stand tall. You can design your future focus on what you have and what you were gifted by God."

She became calm.

I asked her, "What do you think about yourself now?"

She said, "I can win!" She was hopeful again. It is easy to lose hope, but when you become hopeful, even a mountain can be moved.

When Moses struggled with his identity, and asked from God, "Who am I?"

God responded; it doesn't matter who you are, I am with you.

Exodus (3:12)

It is very important that you know that you are not alone.

Today I feel that my adversities have strengthened me. I didn't feel so when I underwent them.

Disney was fired, and went bankrupt. He once said, "All the adversities I've had in my life, and all my troubles and obstacles have strengthened me. You may not realize it when it happens, but a kick in the teeth may be the best thing in the world for you."

I began a journey, travelled through my old patterns of thinking, and said, "It is high time to say good bye to you. Enough is enough! I want to clear my path towards success. I want to replace my 'can't' things on the outside with 'can' things within. In other words, I don't want to think about what I don't have. I want to focus on what I really have in me." Thus, I took control over myself, and empowered my mind by instilling a fresh set of thoughts.

1. I found reasons as to why I have to win in my life.

   Compelling reasons, burning reasons, emotional reasons!

   I lost some opportunities in my life due to my father's death. Whatever I couldn't achieve in my life, I want to give to my son. I wanted to do my MBA from a reputed university overseas; I wanted to be a cricketer; I wanted to go to a city school and study in the English medium. I lost everything. Now my son is studying in one of the best International colleges in Sri Lanka; he practices tennis, cricket, football, golf and speaks five languages. I want to send him to Harvard University for higher education.

I want to give my mum the best medical facilities in future and keep her alive until I achieve a very remarkable goal in my life, which is set to come true in 2034. I give her the best nutritional supplements in the world. There are a handful of people who helped me when I was down, and I want to repay them with gratitude in the most excellent way possible.

2. The real purpose in my life:

   I believe my country deserves my service in a different manner. I want to serve my country. People who challenged me, toughened me; their obdurate natures helped me to become a tough guy. The rivers, canals, water, trees, wind, rain, sunlight and rocks helped me. As a mischievous boy, I enjoyed them all.

3. Gifts and talents:

   Creativity, a fine voice, writing skill, organizing skill, leadership gifts - I found all these in me, gifts created by my God. Using them, I have to celebrate Him. I don't want to carry even one talent without releasing it gloriously for the benefit of my generation and this planet.

4. My characteristics /values:

   I'm punctual and unselfish, and enjoy revealing my efforts. I believe that if I show more patience at this moment that will enhance my talents. Earlier I misused my talents due to a lack of tolerance and self discipline. It doesn't mean that you should not take risks in life, as long as they are legitimate, legal and ethical. Playing in casinos granted me only stupidity and led me to take risks in unworthy things.

5. The moral and ethical literacy, which I own, is more significant than my college degrees. They are my most valuable assets to achieve my success, much more than the paper and professional qualifications which I possess. I have a heart full of generosity. I believe that once I master one branch, I can achieve avalanches of abundance in my life. I should use them not merely for self cause but instead, benefit many in society.

You too can find some reasons and qualities in yourselves; they will surely be the investors in your living enterprise.

Write about one person and four things that you feel that you have:

1. Person

   You should have someone that you are emotionally attached to. If you feel that you are alone, limiting factors will surround you. Very rarely did someone achieve something extraordinary without having anyone special in life. Behind most of the great achievers, there was a woman. If you don't have anyone, find someone. Great company will give great results. You can be emotionally attached to God before all. He can be your paradise, father and provision.

2. Talent

   Everyone possesses talents; find one in you. Sharpen it until you get mastery over it.

3. Quality

   Stick to the qualities you have. Don't compromise for short runs, but shake off short term benefits. If you don't have any good quality, then learn and practice. All skills and qualities are learnable, if you have the mindset to do so.

4. Connection

   Connect with God. If you have that connection, all other relations can be made quickly.

5. Environment.

   Family, work and social environments are all vital. If they do not advance you, make a shift.

Memory count

1. When you step into anything new, a job or business, step in with the belief that you 'can'. Until you cement that 'can' factor, don't move. If you do something with doubt or you do nothing at all, you will have similar kind of results. 'Can't' is the worst limiting factor, which doesn't allow you to move. It proves that you don't have self confidence, without which nothing will progress.
2. Concentrate on what you have in your hand, and don't be greedy over the fruits in others' hands. They will never fill your tummy.
3. Don't mourn for what you couldn't complete or for what you missed. They are in the past and you can't drag them forth as you have no power over them. Never get stuck in the jungle roads where buses never travel.

4. Don't get discouraged when others overtake you. If you try to compete with others, your self esteem will plummet. If you want to be better than you were yesterday, compete with yourself, and go back to analyze your drawbacks. Even though you crawl forward today, tomorrow you will be able to stand and walk.
5. Some people turn immune to unnecessary relations. If you get immune to work that you don't like, hidden damages will be caused. If your relationship is torturing and bothering you constantly, take prompt action. If you don't like your boss, leave and find a better place to work in. The next decade is ready to welcome more home based businesses. Do something radical. All those who are in the top today risked many things to get there.
6. Find reasons to live life, and live life to the hilt. Life is not an accident. It's a purposeful journey mapped out by your creator. Give up extreme greed, and gather up all the fullness.
7. Give gratitude to everyone and everything that helped you when you were down. When you are in the top, don't hide away from them, but acknowledge their contributions.
8. Encouraging words have more power than the money in your pocket. You can motivate someone for a better cause and show them something that they can't see. If you can see yourself clearly, then you can see the others around you, and make them understand their grants and blessings.
9. You can lose control, but don't lose your qualities. Even if you lose all your material things, safeguard your noble qualities, for you can bounce back for sure and hold your head up among others.
10. Expand your vision. Look ahead, plan for the decades and work on it. If you have long term perspectives, there are better chances that you will attain your highest level than those who have shorter dimensions.
11. Take decisions quickly; maybe your decisions today might be wrong, but eventually, the right decisions will come along when you take them.
12. Keep somebody or something behind the screen, while focusing on your dreams, and move forward to experience the amazing back up power you receive, when your battery is down.

24

Can you give me your spirit?

While doing a multilevel marketing business in India, my personality was exposed more than in the previous businesses that I was engaged in. There were a few reasons for that. The unlimited potential offered by this business opportunity, convinced me that I should stretch myself. Even though I felt uncomfortable facing numerous challenges, the big picture of a luxurious lifestyle engraved in my mind, made me obsess. Vivid compelling pictures that I saw in my mental eye drove me on to make vigorous efforts without poring over future effects that could turn negative.

Big dreams, huge pictures and an opulent lifestyle had always shone in my mind. Even while facing many objections and rejections, I moved forward, having grasped the essence of an amazing business model, which was still too much in its formative stage for common acceptance as a legitimate and workable system.

Surprisingly, in this business, few like, many doubt, many join, few do, many fail, and few win. People find this business very different from the other existing businesses. In any business, many fail, and few win. That is the nature of business.

One day I made an appointment with a new prospect, who was a financial adviser and trainer. He had tried this business previously but hadn't focused fully on it. He made no comment or interruption while I presented my plan. He paid close attention to my business proposal, and finally asked, "Can you give me your spirit?"

I smiled, as he said, "Seriously, you have an amazing spirit."

Back home, I sat before my computer, and checked the dictionary. In Latin 'spirit' means "breathe", "like breathing". If your spirit sags, you miss the life force. Very true! Many people live, but miss the life force. My prospect was correct. I have that life force! It shows on the impressions on my face, words and actions. Who controls this breathing? All vital functions in our body including breathing, the heartbeat and healing processes are controlled by the creative intelligence, connected with supernatural power. These are beyond our conscious control and align with the invisible power.

Why do some people have a higher level of spirit than others? The reason is that many don't understand the power of creative intelligence, and how to connect with the infinite creative power. It's very simple; the bridge is faith, and when you believe that miraculously, God's power is working in you, you begin to work enthusiastically and passionately in all departments of your life. This creates noticeable and significant changes in your life, drawing the attention of others, and causing people to remark that you have an amazing spirit.

This spirit can draw forth abundance in all areas of your life. Health, wealth, and happiness are magnificently available for you. When spirit flows, there are no doubts and no fears. You will be a confident person. Even though temporary setbacks appear, they will flee away, bringing forth glory through the connectivity that you strengthen with God.

The Lord shall preserve you from all evil. He shall preserve your soul. The Lord shall preserve your going out and coming in from this time forth, and even forevermore.

Psalm 121:7

Evil things point to possible defeats, harm and danger. When He preserves your soul, the soul will connect with the spirit of the Lord. By knowing the Lord, praising the Lord, believing in the Lord and meditating on prayers for the Lord, you will cultivate all the positive possibilities. You have the fortitude to fight back even if you are stuck in the greatest battle in life.

Lift up your eyes on high. And see who has created these things.

Isaiah 40:26

When you lift up your eyes and see, you will be connected with the creator. How do you get this connectivity? It's through the spirit which transforms the energy through the creative intelligence into your subconscious mind. In order to attract this power, you have to consciously believe and get wired with God.

Simple faith - when I do good I feel good, when I do bad I feel bad. And that is my religion.

Abraham Lincoln

This is one way to be spirited; keeping your self esteem high by doing good things according to your faith.

You are not here merely to make a living. You are here in order to enable the world to live more amply, with greater vision, with a finer spirit of hope and achievement. You are here to enrich the world, and you impoverish yourself if you forget the errand.

Woodrow Wilson

Never be in a hurry; do everything quietly and in a calm spirit. Do not lose your inner peace for anything whatsoever, even if your whole world seems upset.

Saint Francis de Sales

Computers are magnificent tools for the realization of our dreams, but no machine can replace the human spark of spirit, compassion, love, and understanding.

Louis V. Gerstner, Jr.

The secret of genius is to carry the spirit of the child into old age, which means never losing your enthusiasm.

Aldous Huxley

Human spirit is the ability to face the uncertainty of the future with curiosity and optimism. It is the belief that problems can be solved, differences resolved. It is a type of confidence. And it is fragile. It can be blackened by fear and superstition.

Bernard Beckett

25

Heading towards Belief

Believe nothing - where ever you read it, whoever said it, no matter if I said it unless it agrees with your own reasons and common sense.

Buddha

We were heading to a city from a rural polling centre, passing small villages. Both sides of the roads were filled with well grown trees and bushes. Images of a dangerous experience crept into my mind, like the coming attractions of a show. Suddenly our motorcade stopped. I was in the front seat of my Mitsubishi Pajero jeep. There were around five or six vehicles ahead of us, with the same number of cars and vans behind us, carrying more than 30 supporters, including my body guards. I can remember one guy who stood up in front of the vehicle that I was sitting in, and hit the windscreen with a big stone. His target was to harm me. Fortunately, even though the glass was shattered, the rock didn't hit me. I understood that we were under attack by the ruling party members, and more than 200 people had surrounded our vehicles, wanting to attack us with swords and iron poles.

I got down from the vehicle while my body guards tried to protect me. Our supporters tried their best to retaliate. One guy came to me with a big sword, trying to target my head, when somebody quickly pushed me aside. One of my supporters was injured. It was really like a war. I realized instantly we would end up with very bad injuries, with even the possibility of losing our lives if the situation continued. I immediately commanded my body guards. They did their level best to take the situation under control.

Being the candidate of an election, I was not provided official security or arms. More than 21 people got injured, one seriously. I saw a blood spot on my shirt and thought it was due to a gunshot. But when I checked it properly, I realized that it had spilled from someone else's injury. I escaped without even a single minor injury while standing in a rain of live bullets.

It was my blind faith in a small pendent which I was wearing. I felt it had the power to protect me from any danger. A person used some very old chants, and warned me that I would be in great danger in this election. For my safety, I had to wear the pendant given by him. I attended some poojas conducted by him and blindly believed in his words. Today I don't believe that black magic has any power. I was blind in my belief, and I believed, without any virtual evidence of any power, in that necklace. I didn't allow my brain to argue with my belief. Belief, without any science, saved my life.

The Buddha's preaching is scientific and convinces even modern knowledgeable people to understand and logically believe in things due to the information and evidences loaded in the rational part of their minds. The fact is that the Buddha's teaching mainly focused on thoughts and mindful actions, and not the sensitive emotions of the heart. He emphasized the cause and effect doctrine, giving no chance for blind belief. Belief in something should agree with reasoning. His philosophical thinking persuades us to realize and to live life with principles. I agree with that. If we could think clearly, our rational mind would find more space to comprehend things carefully.

In this chapter, my intention flows towards beliefs, stressing their importance without categorizing or underestimating the nature of any belief. People have different kinds of beliefs. According to my sense and personal experience, every belief has power and leads to some results. A very strong belief will lead to enormous results. If it is a little one, you will get little results. I believe that every belief will generate energy of some sort, as long as it does not cause harm to anyone.

The Bible says

If his son asks him for bread, will the father give him a stone?

If you believe and ask for what you really want, instead of the good thing that you ask, you will not be provided with bad results.

Malpensa Airport

It was one afternoon in 2010. I was trying to collect the documents that had fallen down from my file before the immigration counter at Malpensa airport, Italy.

"Signore cos'è successo?"

The Immigration officer asked, "What happened?"

I smiled and gave him my passport

"Vai a casa?" – "Are you going home?"

"Si!" "Yes!"

He stamped the passport and cleared my exit, without checking anything. I had a letter to be submitted to him, but I didn't give it. It was not a spontaneous, isolated incident. If he had checked my details carefully, I would not have been allowed to exit because there was a case filed against me, with a possibility that I would be sent to jail for at least seven years.

I didn't do anything wrong, I was used by someone, an Italian citizen, who was responsible for all the wrong doing, but he had escaped from the case using his contacts. His name was Guido, and he had acted as a lawyer, cheated me of my money and got me into trouble. He was clever enough to arrange some evidence against me and another Sri Lankan guy, who ran the counseling office in Milan.

I stayed in Italy for two years on a temporary refugee permit. I worked for someone who was running a counseling office. We did the necessary paper work, especially for Sri Lankans.

My application for refugee status was turned down and I made an appeal to the courts. After a few months, it was turned down again. I had to exit from the country but due to the case, I was not legally allowed to.

But I knew the consequences if I stayed further, and decided to exit anyhow.

I didn't have any option even though I was born a Buddhist. I was told by my close friend about a church which gives amazing miracles for believers. I went there and simply offered my petition to God. I had no idea about the church or its religious practices. I hadn't even read The Bible. I just believed what my friend told me and constantly prayed until my departure. A small booklet, which I was given by my friend, nestled in my pocket, as I believed that it would give me protection from all. It was really a miracle. Belief appeared as an invisible power and allowed me to exit from Italy without being convicted.

I was born a Buddhist. In our country, the majority practice Buddhism mixed with the concept of God. Pure 'Theravāda' does not exist and I could not find someone who followed that doctrine. Buddhism is not a religion that has a belief in supernatural things; it's a teaching. It teaches how to live in peace and find the path to end this life cycle, preventing rebirth. We believe in some Sri Lankan Gods and some Hindu Gods. Being a Buddhist, I don't see any fault in this.

There is a place which is believed to have been visited by the Buddha called Sripada, Adams peak. Many Buddhists believe that some Gods protect that area and that when we go there, we can get their blessings. There is another place called Kataragama where God Skanda Kumara lives. These are all beliefs but those who believe, get results.

She spoke again

In 1990, we went on an educational trip from our school to visit several places in Sri Lanka. One place among those was called Kataragama. One of my cousin sisters, who was studying in our school, suddenly became mute a few months back. She couldn't talk for months, and not even one word came out from her mouth. The doctors couldn't find any reasons for this medical condition, and she and her family members were very worried. She also joined us on the trip. Everyone was amazed as she spoke exactly when we reached that sacred place. Wasn't it a miracle? We were all happy, and she explained that she had believed strongly that she would be able to speak when she reached there. Her belief worked. I witnessed it myself.

If we had some promises to be fulfilled, and nobody took the initiative to go to that Mandir (sacred place), people believed that that is why troubles came again and again. The Gods were not happy with us. How many times did children get unwell! It was common in our house, and my grandma complained. Not only she, but many believed that there were numerous places to be worshipped for many reasons. I experienced it many times when we collectively participated to fulfill the promises of the said Gods, after which we enjoyed better periods than before in every aspect.

Then we could hear our happy grandma's voice, full of spirit and enthusiasm. Many live because of their beliefs.

My knee was healed

I was walking down the street of Crocetta, in Milan to catch the metro at Crocetta metro station. Suddenly I felt a sharp pain in my knee and I couldn't walk any more. I leant against the wall of a shop, keeping my full body weight on one leg. After some time, the pain subsided and I could continue my walking. This knee pain developed gradually till it was hard to climb steps in the metros and at home. I was really worried and in panic, because I was a man full of aspirations and dreams. I didn't want to have anything negative in me.

When I was in Milan, Italy, the only friend who stood by me, protected me, fed me, accompanied me in spiritual journeys and always ignited hopes in me, was Davina. Indeed, she became my second mum. Up to date, and forever, we share all the things, whether in happiness or in sorrow. Many may appear in the future like her, but she will remain, without any replacement, as the number one angel sent by God to be my guardian.

We went to the hospital and underwent some tests, and the doctors advised me to undergo a knee surgery to cure the pain. I had been petrified of operations since my childhood, because I saw my mother and close relatives who underwent surgeries, suffering for months.

Though the technology in Italy is very high in comparison with Sri Lanka, I didn't give my consent for the operation of my knee. Even my friend advised against it. She believed that this too would pass.

Whenever I passed churches, without any consideration of their religious practices, I would enter, kneel down and speak to God.

"God, I have so many things to do; look after my son and loved ones.

I am full of dreams to be accomplished; heal me, and please allow this pain to pass soon, and make me walk again like before."

After a few weeks, without any treatment, my leg became normal. I could walk again like before, even run and climb steps fast. Everybody was amazed. It was my belief, I know! No words more than that! I can't explain exactly how long you have to hold onto what you believe in, to get the results. I assume that the duration would not be long if your heart accepts your belief blindly with all its emotions.

Belief is one of the key factors in success. It is not just the main one; it is the only one which kick starts the process of achieving success. Even though you fulfill all the other requirements to achieve something that you want, without belief, things will not work out.

If you have belief in a superior power other than you, like God, religion or universal power, it will strengthen your level of confidence. Confidence doesn't come from body muscles. It is born in the mind. When you have belief and faith in your mind, it automatically creates a spirit in you.

Spirit creates enthusiasm. If you embrace enthusiasm, you allow supernatural power to engender in you, and if you hold on to it, you will become enthusiastic. It generates creativity in you, and that creativity itself makes ideas that create wonders in your life.

I believe in Jesus Christ as my Lord and savior. I believe that Jesus died for my sins, and rose again, and that's my belief. I still don't know what 'Christian' means. I'm a follower of Christ, but I keep making a whole bunch of mistakes. And I thank God for forgiveness.

Sherri Shepherd

It's the repetition of affirmations that leads to belief. And once that belief becomes a deep conviction, things begin to happen.

Muhammad Ali

The special forces gave me the self-confidence to do some extraordinary things in my life. Climbing Everest then cemented my belief in myself.

Bear Grylls

A wise man proportions his belief to the evidence.

David Hume

Memory count

1. Belief is one of the vital building blocks that can build and strengthen your confidence. It's like a cornerstone. If a cornerstone is not strong, the structure will not be long lasting, and can fall down at any moment
2. It is important to believe in something, rather than living without any belief. Nihilists don't trust anything. What you believe is not important. Even blind belief can bring forth expected results in an incredible way.
3. When you establish your faith, believing in someone or something and yourself, as a result, you get an amazing level of confidence to move forward. Believing in God, religious teachings, rituals and customs, the power of the universe, and the power of the mind, all give enormous support to live a confident life in peace and happiness, driving towards success in any area of life that you deserve.
4. Sometimes we have to believe in leaders in a particular field, mentors and coaches, at other times in systems; if you are in a business which has some models and systems, you have to believe in them single-mindedly to avoid distractions.

   For example; the multilevel marketing business! It's quite a revolutionary business model, but not everyone will realize its importance and follow it.
5. Why some people do not get results from medicine is because they don't believe that the medicine can help them. But see some pills advertised in the media rigorously for headaches, and people get quick results in many cases. The reason is established belief through strong conviction. Some supplements have the amazing power to reduce weight and flatten stomachs. I experienced them myself. But the

same dietary supplements used by one of my friends didn't get him satisfactory results as he didn't believe that he could lose weight.

6. When you believe in positive things, they will surely attract you through the law of attractions. People who achieve success all of a sudden, in the same level as you, or lower, magnetize and accumulate what they need through these secrets. Principles, rules, and fundamentals are freely available and they will work for you if you believe in them.
7. Believe that superior and invisible powers are working in you and can protect you and supply your needs. When the level of your human power goes down, those powers will lift you up provided you have a strong conviction.
8. Many of us believe things we catch through our five senses, which is why people tend to repeat the same experience again. If someone has failed earlier, based on past results, they are reluctant to fight back again. But people, who understand and believe in their sixth sense, reveal no doubt and fear. They will bounce back a hundred fold, finding solutions through their creative intelligence. Believe in your creative faculty which lies in your subconscious mind. Many scientists, inventors, artists, singers, great poets, writers and speakers create wonders through this.
9. Some people are energetic, spirited, enthusiastic and passionate workers, while others are not. The difference is the level of confidence that works in them. Confident characters are believers who assume that this world has made a stage for them to play on. There are two great forces which can embrace us when we move forward in progress. One is fear - when it appears, many flee, leaving behind all their big hopes. The second is faith - when it is impregnated, fear will run away, erasing all the shadows which haunt your mind.
10. You may have all the resources, skills, talents, potentialities, but if you don't have faith, you will always be stuck, playing the game within limits. You can begin everything without faith, but be able to complete it a 100% only with faith and belief.
11. Written goals bring you the "I can" belief. Many people fear to write goals and set deadlines because they are not confident about their achievements. Even if you cannot finish the goal according to the deadline, if you can come up with amended strategic plans, you will proceed until you make it. Most people give up or fail because they are

not ready to make constant efforts to replace new plans. If one plan fails, come up with another.

12. Affirm prayers; believe that God loves to see your victory, not your defeat. Don't get discouraged in trials. With term tests you will be qualified for the finals.

If you blindly believe, you can see from your eyes more than you do. That sight itself gives you the foresight to envision your future.

Keerthisinghe

26

If you want to get Success

Success is nothing more than a few simple disciplines, practiced every day.

Jim Rohn

If you really want to be successful, you have to do something that unsuccessful people don't want to do in their lives. Such people do not want to incorporate the factors, elements and fundamentals that are very vital in achieving success. Some people don't see value in their lives, or in the lives of others too. So they don't make any worthy efforts. Sometimes no reasons can be given for their inactions. That is just how they are.

Many unsuccessful people hold within, unbearable and harmful burdens in their lives, without realizing it. Some have emotions that they don't manage. They hate people, live with anger and crave revenge, are jealous of even their loved ones and secretly compete with them. They laugh at the adversity of others, and they enjoy the cruel happiness of criticizing people away from their circle. Gossiping always cultivates misery and they harvest it bountifully. Doubt and fear are their good friends, whose company they enjoy. Their passion is poverty and they live in their prison of comfort. Their art is isolation. Many are shady characters, with negative stories and mysterious things in life. They have no friends or very few. They don't believe in the existence of a power beyond themselves. They campaign negativity and have a negative impact on others' lives. In short, unsuccessful people don't deliver anything good for this planet.

Successful people do completely opposite things from unsuccessful ones. They are men of principles. They are programmed, and they become machines, unstoppable and unreasonable. They never look back, or listen to unsuccessful stories in the past. When the past appears, they let it pass. They believe and trust in secrets, supernatural things, miraculous powers and creative intelligence within. They are ready to change and ready to fail. They don't accept failure as a defeat, but instead accept that delay and come up with new plans and strategies. If new plans fail, they find new ideas and concepts to create another new plan. They never stop, and never falter until they see their accomplishments.

They are passionate, committed and willing to take risks. That's why these people are worthy characters. They discipline themselves, and change those habits and behavior that are not nourishing. They have the courage to stop addictions and practice patience. They keep moving. They don't stay in one level, but always focus on the next level. They understand the value of hard work and they never try to substitute that. They make relations and value them, keeping the fire within always. They read not only books, but minds. They have intuition, they are leaders, organizers, thinkers, dreamers and are never satisfied with what they are, always trying to discover extraordinary things. They are not selfish and offer contributions that are significant, as also flexible, adjustable, stretchable and expandable! Searching and seeking, they never compromise on their dreams. They envision and imagine good things. They start every day as a new day, and live in the future. True successful people develop moral ethical values.

If you represent great ideas and possibilities to become someone, it should be reflected in your behavior, your words in communication, your dress, your friends and associates. You have to act as if:

You want to be a billionaire, showing that keenness in every aspect of your life. You have to live in that dream, organizing all activities around that. If you want to start a business to attract abundance, it should be a feasible project to return your will as you dream of it in your life time. It gives some sort of vibration to your brain to keep you awake in your mission. Your great ideas should be shared with a mastermind of people who can understand and value them. People who want to achieve something in their lives will find driven characters and join them. When you share your hunches, someone may add to their value and come forward to join hands with your idea to give it a life. Don't always think that the world is full of cynical people. There are people of quality, but you have to find them.

Recently, I have asked my heart one question frequently. Why I can't be what I really want to be in my life? I can't see the reasons which prevent me from becoming what I want to be. Of course I have to convey what I really want to my creative faculty within, and cooperate with my conscious and subconscious mind. For, unless I have the support of my invisible means, it will not be possible. I also have to chalk out a definite time to achieve those tasks. When I make it a habit to consume fewer calories, my stomach gets used to it after some days. Likewise, my mind also takes some time to make it a habit. After that, at unexpected moments, it delivers the results. What I want to achieve in life someone already has achieved on this planet. I don't believe only super successful people possess that greatness. Why can't I be the next? Everyone is gifted and possesses more than one calling, or talent. If we could master that or have the capacity to handle the people who hold the mastery of knowledge, we can be what we truly want to be. Several material aids can be used to get useful insights which have all been shared by successful people in particular areas. I want to be one of the bestselling authors, as also one of the best speakers on this planet. I also want to own an abundance of money and luxuries with a fulfilling relationship, contribute a larger amount to this planet, and live life with significance and style.

My friend**'s investment on his marriage**

One day, one of my friends came to my place, looking depressed. His face was pale, his beard was not shaved and his hair was untidy. His dress was not pressed. He asked for some water while entering the house. Though I realized that something was wrong, I didn't ask. He sat on the sofa, and asked if anyone was at home. I said, "No!" He started to cry, which upset me. He was a strong guy and I had never seen him so broken. He disclosed the whole story.

His wife had cheated on him on several occasions. When he got to know it for the first time, he was shocked and devastated. When she got caught, she asked him to pardon her, promising that she would not to repeat the mistake. He believed her. But again and again, she did the same thing, asking for pardon each time she got caught.

He told me he had spent more than ten years with her, doing everything that she wanted, including spending money on a luxury vacation until his credit cards had got maxed out. He threw a grand wedding, and bought a house in her name. All his credit cards had supplementary cards in her name. Fixed deposits and investments were all jointly done. The only thing he didn't share was her extramarital affair.

He expected an opinion from me as a reliable friend.

I said that if the situation was as true as he had described, he needed to get a divorce. He couldn't make up his mind because he had done so many things for her. I told him to forget about all that. "Think about the future. Relationships should be nourishing. If they hand you worries, they slow you down. Sometimes the end can be disastrous. Being an educated guy, you have to think about this. What will happen to the children? You have to break down the complexity of your problem and troubleshoot one by one, according to the priorities. You might not get all the answers right now. This is life. You are not the only one who is facing this. There are many people who have undergone similar issues. Think about the future and expect something good is going to happen to you."

He said he drank a lot these days. I said, "Think clearly without excessive alcohol." I recommended some books related to how to maintain good relationships. I advised him that the decision should be made according to his consciousness, and not the opinion of others. "Listen to your heart. Ask for the way out. It's personal, and only your heart knows the road map. Because of the size of the pain and nature of the cause, your heart knows what you have lost and what you are going to further lose. You have to measure which one is greater in size!"

He seemed consoled.

After a few months, another friend of mine called me to speak about the friend who had come to meet me several months ago. I went to see him in jail. He had killed his wife and her paramour. He didn't talk much, only a few words. He drove his life to darkness. The way he responded to the event resulted in this tragedy. When situations and circumstances appear, how we respond to them can bring about a constructive or a destructive outcome. We may not understand when it happens, because we feel that there are no other options to solve the matter. We are emotionally overwhelmed and react. The results are not good for the future and remain as unpleasant patches.

My friend came out from jail after three months, and the case was over as he managed to prove an exception in law, and sudden provocation. The law released him, but the negative effects of the action were not over. The children would suffer. He would also suffer and live with regrets.

We should not do something that we will regret in our lives. When we want to make a decision, even though it is hard, we have to choose that hard decision. Temporarily you might be defeated. But in the long run, you will have options and better choices. If he had got the divorce, the outcome would have been completely different. He could have married again. The children would have had a mum again. He would not be a murderer. My friend became mentally unstable after a few months and committed suicide. The children lost their father too.

Memory Count

1. Resolve to get success in all areas of your life.
2. Every subject has principles; success is a subject to learn. Follow the principles, and the results will follow.
3. Notice the characteristics of successful people and apply them in your life, if you lack them presently.
4. Don't think that the world is full of cynical people. Look for good people; you will surely meet them.
5. No matter how much time and money you lose, if your relationship is draining, quit immediately.
6. Successful people never let emotions override their souls. Don't react with emotions, but learn to manage them.
7. Successful people never carry temporary defeats along their life. They focus on long term victories.
8. Don't get discouraged in the first attempt. In every area of life, personal, professional and spiritual, you will get several chances.
9. Be an optimist, and never let sinful thoughts erase your qualities.
10. Maintain a balance sheet of your life, with credits and debits.
11. We are born with joy, live and achieve things with joy, and leave with joy.
12. Nothing is unbearable in life. Expect to bear fruits that can be enjoyed by yourself and others.

Coming together is a beginning; keeping together is progress; working together is success.

Henry Ford

The price of success is hard work, dedication to the job at hand, and the determination that whether we win or lose, we have applied the best of ourselves to the task at hand.

Vince Lombardi

Man needs his difficulties because they are necessary to enjoy success.

A. P. J. Abdul Kalam

Success is not the key to happiness. Happiness is the key to success. If you love what you are doing, you will be successful.

Albert Schweitzer

27

Affirm your Prayer

Billions of people pray every day to receive things according to their heart's desires. Most of the time we pray when we are in danger, or when obstacles and problems block our boundaries.

We want to have happier, healthier and richer lives. Many prayers are not answered; sometimes you don't get results according to your wish. If you really want to get answers for your prayer, affirm your prayer scientifically. Scientific is, according to late Latin, 'Scientificus'. 'Producing knowledge' from Sciencia is an art. What kind of knowledge do you have to produce?

Lord Buddha preached Vidya. In Sanskrit, Vidya is knowledge. Even when you pray for better results, you should do it with proper knowledge. When you pray, you should know how to pray.

Many of us ask for things from our prayers rigorously. Over days, months and years, some pray, doing unbearable sacrifices, and even torturing their bodies!

No matter who you believe in or what religion you follow, you can pray to get answers for your request. Your heart is not only a blood pumping organ, but a place where your soul and the mind connect. The heart plays a vital and tremendous role in prayer. Don't allow your brain to dominate your emotions; let them flow and bring wonders through prayer.

Steps:

1. Cleanse yourself

   Many people do this before prayer. If you are tired and sweating, you will not feel good about yourself. A good feeling in your body makes your mind fresh, energetic and positive. When you feel good, good things attract you, according to the law of attraction.

2. Be relaxed.

   Stay in a serene and quiet environment. With noise, you can't concentrate on anything. Proper concentration will align and combine with straight miraculous energies.

3. Connect with your God or belief, and build your faith, praising and admiring with gratitude the wonders He has created. This working power, filled with wonder, can heal the blind, the dumb and even the paralyzed.

   Present your case with emotions and feelings. If you want to get a job, feel that it has been received. Make a mental picture of the happy moment and tightly hold it. Be aware and be sure of the answer. Have no doubts.

4. Be specific and reasonable:

   Don't complicate your request. At one time, focus on one prayer. Be firm about the request. Don't ask for someone else's property or money. You will not feel good about yourself and it will lead to the answer - 'NO'.

5. Prioritize your prayer.

   According to your need, prioritize it. If you need good health, pray first to gain that, without asking for a promotion in your job.

6. Plant your prayer in your deep mind (subconscious) as a picture. Visualize images of happy answering and feel it, hear the noise, smell the fragrance, use your five senses and allow your sixth sense to awake with the creation of a solution.

7. Nurture your prayer and be honest.

   Practice it frequently and stick to it honestly.

8. Sacrifice or Fast

   You need to sacrifice your addictions, joy or passion fully or temporarily. Harvest

9. Receive a smooth answer.

Prayer is not asking. It is a longing of the soul. It is daily admission of one's weakness. It is better in prayer to have a heart without words than words without a heart.

Mahatma Gandhi

Thank you' is the best prayer that anyone could say. I say that one a lot. Thank you expresses extreme gratitude, humility, understanding.

Alice Walker

There are many things that are essential to arriving at true peace of mind, and one of the most important is faith, which cannot be acquired without prayer.

John Wooden

I do believe we're all connected. I do believe in positive energy. I do believe in the power of prayer. I do believe in putting good out into the world. And I believe in taking care of each other.

Harvey Fierstein

God, our Creator, has stored within our minds and personalities, great potential strength and ability. Prayer helps us tap and develop these powers.

A. P. J. Abdul Kalam

About the Author

Keerthisinghe, Sri Lankan in origin, based in India, is an entrepreneur, speaker, politician and T.V. Presenter. He possesses sound knowledge of Buddhist philosophy and is a great man of God.

At the age of eight he lost his pillar, his father, and struggled a lot, facing numerous challenges in life. While amidst many difficulties, he entered the University of Colombo, and graduated as a Bachelor of Laws, and in 2000, acquired the professional qualifications of a lawyer. During his childhood, in school, he revealed his inborn talent for poetry, (the first copy of his poetry book was presented to the then president of Sri Lanka) sports and debates. Due to the few facilities he had, he could not reach the expected levels. He lost myriad opportunities in life.

He failed many times in life; sometimes he was blessed with all the luxuries and at other times, he had to settle with the basics.

When he was in office as a member of the provincial council from 2004–2008, he was very regular and a famous face in T.V. debates. In his early thirties he became a rupee multi-millionaire and then again, lost everything he had.

He is unstoppable, and he is still on his quest.

In his early forties, he discovered his purpose in life, and mastered his self-values. This book is a trademark of his amazing spirit and he is working on his second manuscript. His dream is to complete all the tasks he began in every area of life and to unleash his talents for the betterment of society.